THE GOLDEN BOOK OF
VENICE

220 Colour illustrations

BONECHI

© Copyright by CASA EDITRICE BONECHI, via Cairoli 18/b Firenze - Italia
Tel +39 055 576841 - Fax +39 055 5000766
E-mail: bonechi@bonechi.it Internet: www.bonechi.it www.bonechi.com

Printed in Italy by Centro Stampa Editoriale Bonechi, Sesto Fiorentino.

ISBN 88-7009-687-4

CREDITS

Photographs from the Archives of Casa Editrice Bonechi, taken by:

Paolo Giambone: pages 1, 5, 8b, 9, 10, 11a, 12b, 13, 14, 19, 26, 27b, 29b, 30, 31, 32b, 33, 44b, 45/51, 53a, 54, 55, 56a, 57b, 58/63, 64a, 65/68, 70/74, 75a, 76/80, 84, 89c, 90/97, 98a, 98b, 99a, 99b, 102, 103b, 103c, 104, 122a.

Gaetano Barone: pages 8, 11, 12a, 16, 17, 27a, 29a, 32a, 40, 44a, 52, 53b, 56b, 57a, 64b, 75b, 81, 82, 86, 89a, 98c, 100b, 103a, 105/107, 124/127.

Gianni Dagli Orti: pages 6, 15, 18, 20, 21, 22/25, 28, 34/39, 41/43, 87, 100a, 101, 108/121, 122b, 123.

Photographs kindly provided by the Azienda di Promozione Turistica di Venezia and taken by:

Renato Boscolo: pag. 85.

Aerial photographs I-BUGA - Aut. SMA n. 506/85: pages 7, 69, 83, 88.

* * *

INTRODUCTION

Water-girt Venice rises on an archipelago of small islands separated by a dense network of waterways, which were rectified as time passed, noticeably changing the original conformation. Venice lies four kilometers from the mainland and two from the open sea.

The original inhabited nucleus of the city took shape during the barbarian invasions when groups of refugees from Spina, Aquileia, Adria, Altino, Padua settled on the islands in the lagoon. In the course of the centuries the population kept increasing, developing into a city the likes of which is not to be found anywhere in the world.

It must also be kept in mind that since over 160 waterways have been covered with earth, the number of islands on which Venice stands has been reduced to eighteen, inclusive of San Giorgio Maggiore and the Giudecca.

The longest of the canals (3.8 km.) and the widest (from 30 to 70 m.) is the Grand Canal which divides the city into two parts that are interconnected by three bridges: the Bridge of the Scalzi, the Bridge of Rialto and that of the Accademia. Forty-five rii or internal canals run into the Grand Canal and they can all be navigated with small boats or gondolas. As many as 350 bridges connect the various zones of the city. The territory is subdivided into sestrieri or districts: Cannaregio, San Marco, Castello, Dorsoduro, San Polo, Santa Croce. Until 1480 the bridges were in wood; later they were replaced by arched stone structures.

Land travel moves over spaces that have their own specific names.

There are not many main streets, rughe (from the French rue) and the salizade or first streets in the city to be paved (selciate). The smaller alleys are called cale or calle while those that run close to the canals and serve as foundations for the houses are known as fondamenta; the lista is that stretch of road next to an ambassadorial residence which enjoyed a particular diplomatic immunity. In addition there are the mercerie, streets lined by shops of various kinds, the rive which are stretches of fondamenta along the rii, the smaller waterways, and more specifically the steps which lead to the water from the fondamenta. Rii tera are filled-in canals, the rami are short stretches of road that branch off from a calle or a campiello. The campo is the square near a church, a large area of open ground once cultivated, mostly as a vegetable garden or used to pasture horses. The campiello is the smaller open space between the houses, to which the calli lead. The small open areas surrounded by buildings and with only one entrance/exit are known as corti. Paludo is the name given to those spaces where there was once a swamp (palude) while the pissine are on the sites of pools where it was possible to fish and swim. What else makes Venetian toponomy unique and an abbreviated survey of history and town-planning? The sotoportego, a stretch of road that passes under the buildings and connects calli, campielli, corti... and then the « canals », waterways, but not by any means minor « ways » of communication — Anything but...!

On the same level as the toponomy, telling the tale of the town- planning history of the city, but the bane of anyone who is not a born Venetian, are the house numbers. The houses are progressively numbered, but according to district and not distinguished into calli, campi, campielli... It was this need to put some order into the confused state of affairs in the city that led to an initial regular numbering of the houses in 1801. This was not however progressive for sestieri, but for the zona de citra and de ultra, on this side and that of San Marco, so that the zone of de citra includes Castello, San Marco and Cannaregio and de ultra Santa Croce, Dorsoduro and San Polo.

Between 1837 and 1941 a survey by districts was instituted and the « black numbers » were replaced by « red » ones. Even so, in certain areas of Venice it is still possible to see examples of « local » numbers in Roman numerals next to the regular numbers in Arab numbers. And sometimes the Roman numerals are written backwards, as in the sotoportego degli Armeni at St. Mark's, where the house numbers 963-964 on one building are flanked by the letters IIIIV and IIIV which stand for IX and VIII.

Basically Venice today still looks as it did in the 13th century, with the exception of a few transformations in various buildings which however play an unimportant part in the general layout of the city plan.

It was not until the 19th century that the need to facilitate communications with the Mainland, and the constant growth in population, led to a few particularly important changes. Connections with the Mainland in fact improved and were speeded up thanks to the construction of the railroad bridge (1841-46) which with its 3,601 meters joins water-girt Venice to Mestre. The road bridge, opened almost a century later, in 1933, now also makes it possible to reach the Mainland by car.

Insular Venice covers an area of a little over seven square kilometers, inclusive of the islands of San Giorgio and the Giudecca.

The area that falls under the jurisdiction of the Commune of Venice is much larger, comprising other important inhabited centers: the islands of Murano, Burano and Torcello, inside the lagoon, the Lido and Pellestrina towards the sea, Malcontenta, Dese, Tessera, Mestre and Marghera, Zelarino, Carpenedo, Asseggiano, Trivignano, Favaro and Chirignago in the immediate hinterland. Some of these places were once autonomous communes.

Two views of Piazza San Marco, the heart of Venice.

PIAZZA SAN MARCO

A gem among gems in the field of Italian architecture, the Piazza San Marco consists of two large contiguous areas: the Piazza itself and its extension, the Piazzetta, which runs down to the sea. Unrivalled examples of architecture face out on this large open space on all sides: the **Basilica of San Marco**, the **Palace of the Doges** or Palazzo Ducale, the **Loggetta**, the tall **Clock Tower**.

The original layout of the Piazza dates to the 9th cent. A.D., and it is essentially still the same despite the various changes that have been made throughout the centuries. As early as the second half of the 12th century Doge Sebastiano Ziani modified the piazza, doubling the space in front of the Basilica, and setting up the two large monolithic columns which ideally close off the Piazzetta. A century later both the Basilica and the Palace of the Doges were variously transformed, and the fortified du-

cal residence became the elegant building with loggias that we see today. At the time, the Piazza was surrounded by interesting buildings such as the headquarters of the Canons of San Marco, the houses of the Procurators, and the Church of San Geminiano, with numerous shops facing out on the Piazzetta. The real transformation of the Piazza began in 1400: many buildings were torn down, the Clock Tower (late 15th cent.) was built, and the Zecca or Mint and the Library were constructed, joined a hundred years later by the Procuratie Nuove. In Sansovino's new project for the Piazza the underlying basic structures followed the original arrangement. At the beginning of the 1700s the centuries-old red brick pavement with its herringbone design was replaced with the grey trachite stone from the Euganean Hills which thousands of visitors still tread under foot today.

CLOCK TOWER

The Clock Tower, built by Codussi between 1496 and 1499, is undoubtedly one of the most photographed monuments in Venice, thanks both to the presence of the original clock and to the two « *Moors* » who strike the hours at the top of the tower. The construction of the lateral parts, designed by P. Lombardo, was begun in 1506 and they were raised higher in 1775 by Giorgio Massari. The bronze « *Moors* » by Ambrogio da le Anchore date to 1497.

Below the Moors is the Lion of San Marco. On the small semicircular terrace further down is a gilt copper statue of the *Madonna and Child* by A. Leopardi and during Ascension week three statues move across the terrace from left to right, passing before the Virgin. The large clock is a masterpiece of clockwork mechanism by Giampaolo and Giancarlo Ranieri from Parma (late 15th cent.), indicating the passing of the seasons, the phases of the moon and the movement of the sun from one sign of the zodiac to the other.

On these pages: various views of the Clock Tower, with the statues of the two Moors who strike the hours.

PROCURATIE VECCHIE AND THE ALA NAPOLEONICA

The fifty round arches which support the two tiers of loggias of the Procuratie Vecchie were built between the end of the 15th and the beginning of the 16th century. M. Codussi worked on the project up to the first floor. The building was finished by B. Bon and G. Grigi, who completed almost all the rest except for the part in the back which was built by Sansovino.

A continuation of the Procuratie Vecchie, on the site of the old church of San Geminiano (demolished in 1807), is the so-called Ala Napoleonica (Napoleonic Wing), built by the French emperor as an enormous ballroom. The ala repeats the two orders of columns of the Procuratie Nuove which Scamozzi built in 1584, inspired by the classical lines of the Libreria Sansoviniana.

PROCURATIE NUOVE

When new premises for the apartments of the nine Procuratori (Magistrates) of San Marco, which were in the Procuratie Vecchie, were needed, Vincenzo Scamozzi was charged with designing the new complex of buildings. He paid little attention to a precedent project by Sansovino and took up the motive of the Libreria Marciana — which is at right angles to the Procuratie — for the two lower floors. He added an upper floor which was also articulated by semicolumns, with tall windows alternately topped by arched and triangular pediments set in between. A molded cornice runs along the entire facade at the top. The old Ospizio Orseolo, whose facade projected further out than the present Procuratie, was demolished and construction work began in 1582 under the direction of Scamozzi. At his death in 1616 work was continued by Carità and then terminated by Longhena. These rooms were turned into the Royal Palace for Napoleon when he was in Venice. Now the nine apartments of the Procuratori, overlooking five inner courtyards, house the **Archaeological Museum**, the **Museo Civico Correr** and the **Museo del Risorgimento**, as well as various municipal offices. The public establishments on the ground floor include, under the portico, the **Caffè Florian**, once the « Venezia trionfante », the meeting place of artists and writers in the 18th and 19th centuries.

◄ *Detail of the Procuratie Vecchie.*

The Procuratie Vecchie and the Ala Napoleonica (Napoleon Wing) on the right; View of the Piazza with the Procuratie Nuove and the Ala Napoleonica, below.

CAMPANILE OF SAN MARCO

The Piazza San Marco is dominated by the lofty bell tower about 100 meters high called « *el paron de casa* » (the master of the house) by the Venetians. But it did not always look like this. In the 9th century, a lookout tower stood on the site which at the time faced directly onto the lagoon since the Piazzetta San Marco (now between the Libreria Marciana and the Palace of the Doges) was a sort of inner harbor. Rebuilt in the second half of the 12th century, two sides of the campanile were at the time set against the buildings which stood in front of the present Procuratie Nuove (the Ospizio Orseolo) and in the area of the Libreria, constituting the corner.

Frequently damaged, it was rebuilt between 1511 and 1514 by Bartolomeo Bon on a project by Giorgio Spavento. Set apart from the adjacent buildings, the shaft of the powerful stocky tower has pilasters up to the arches which make it look like a pier of the classic period. Over the belfry, pierced by four-light openings, is a drum which supports the pyramidal steeple and the statue of the Archangel Gabriel. Inaugurated with great pomp, the structure stood intact until 1902, when it suddenly crumbled. It was decided to rebuild it « *com'era e dov'era* » (as it was and where it was). Reconstruction terminated in 1912, including Sansovino's Loggetta which had been gravely damaged when the bell tower fell. Nowadays, from the belfry where Galileo tried out his telescope, a magnificent panorama can be had over the lagoon and the city as far as the Alps.

SANSOVINO'S LOGGETTA

The Loggetta was designed by Sansovino for the base of the campanile. In the niches the architect placed bronze statues of *Apollo*, *Mercury*, *Peace*, and *Minerva*. The *gate* and the two *putti* on either side of the attic are by A. Gai.

In 1505 A. Leopardo set up three *standard bases* between the Loggia and the Clock Tower to replace their wooden forebears. The one in the center has a medallion with the profile of *Doge L. Loredan*.

Two pictures of the famous Campanile and a detail of Sansovino's graceful Loggetta.

LIBRERIA MARCIANA

The west side of the Piazzetta San Marco is occupied by the Libreria Marciana or Sansovino Library. The palace was destined to house the precious collection of books which Cardinal Bessarione had gratefully donated to the city for having given him asylum when he fled from Nicaea when it was occupied by the Turks. The building, which consists of two stories — a Doric portico and an Ionic upper story —, was commissioned from Sansovino in 1536. Two large caryatids flank the central entrance in the portico. Inside, at the top of a remarkable staircase in two flights which imitates the « golden staircase » in the Doges' Palace, is a vestibule with a splendid ceiling decorated by Stefano and Cristoforo Rosa in the middle of the 16th century.

The library contains outstanding treasures from the Biblioteca Marciana including the famous *Grimani Breviary*, and the known *Mappamento di Fra Mauro* (1549); hundreds of thousands of books; the rare examples of Greek and Latin codexes and the Marini Sanudo's « *Diari* ».

The Zecca or Mint where the famous gold zecchino was coined is also by Sansovino. The palace was taken over by the Libreria Marciana in 1905.

The Libreria Marciana.

Some of the principal monuments in the city look out on the Piazzetta San Marco.

The Basilica of San Marco, the principal monument in the city.

BASILICA OF SAN MARCO

San Marco is the « great temple » of Venice, the monumental symbol not only of the State Church, but of political power as well, for it was originally created as a Ducal Chapel and did not become the seat of the Patriarch until the 19th century. The Procurators of San Marco, entrusted both with the burden and the honor of looking after the Basilica, were not members of the clergy, and the « Primicerio », a noble of the Republic, to whom canons and vicars turned their eyes during the religious rites, was chosen by the doge. San Marco was the heart of the city, the fulcrum around which life in Venice

revolved. It was here that the newly elected doge was solemnly acclaimed and it was in the Basilica that the doge blessed and solemnly saw off those who had been charged with leading the ships and armies of the Most Serene Republic into war.

The *doorways* set into the *facade* of the Basilica of San Marco are five in number, just as there are five cupolas in eastern style which lend both solidity and movement to the structure as a whole. Each of the portals presents specific moments in the story of the *Recovery of the Body of the Evangelist*. Beginning on the right, we have the *Body of St. Mark Stolen from the Infidels*, the *Arrival in Venice of the Mortal Remains of the Saint* (by Pietro

15

Detail of the facade of the Basilica of San Marco.

Detail of the principal portal with the mosaic by Liborio ►
Salandri (1836) depicting Christ in Glory and the Last
Judgement.

Detail of the portal of San Alipio with the mosaic depicting ►
the Translation of the Body of Saint Mark in the Basilica.

16

◄ *Basilica of San Marco, atrium. Above: general view of the left side; below a view of the so-called "Genesis" dome with the mosaics depicting the creation of man and a detail of the same depicting the building of the Tower of Babel.*

General view of the interior.

Vecchia), then the *Venetians Worshipping the Body of St. Mark* (the mosaic is by Sebastiano Ricci), and the *Translation of the Body of St. Mark to the Church*. The central portal is decorated with bas the reliefs in Venetian Romanesque style representing the *Venetian Trades*, the *Months* and the *Virtues*. The large mosaic above is a 19th century work after a cartoon by Lattanzio and depicts the *Last Judgement*.

Further up behind a slender balustrade are copies of the *four horses* attributed to Lysippus, of the 4th century B.C., brought back from Constantinople in 1204 as spoils of war by Doge Enrico Dandolo.

The horses were placed on San Marco in 1250. In 1798 Napoleon took them to Paris as war booty but in 1815 they were returned to Venice thanks to the Austrians. The originals, duly restored, are now inside the church.

Four octagonal columns with 11th-century capitals are installed behind these imposing bronze horses. All the sculpture in the upper part was begun in 1385 by the Dalle Masegne.

The facade that overlooks the *Piazzetta dei Leoncini*, echoes the design of the main facade, with arches and marble statues in the aedicules and gables. The bas reliefs and the water spouts, by Pietro Lamberti, are also quite lovely, as is the elegant *Porta dei Fiori*, inserted in the fourth arcade. Under a large arch on the same side is the *tomb of Daniele Manin*, by Luigi Borro, whose mortal remains were brought back from Paris in 1868.

The lovely Baroque facade (1675) of the ex-church of **San Basso** — attributed to Longhena — also faces onto this square. Inside are the four panels from the organ of San Marco by Giovanni Bellini. At the back of the piazza the neo-classic facade of the **Palazzo Patriarcale**, a 19th-century building by Lorenzo Santi, stands in all its clarity of form.

A spacious **atrium** and a sort of gallery that runs the entire length of the church separate the outside from the inside of the Basilica. These sixty-two meters (6 m. wide and 7.35 m. high) of wall are decorated with columns from various places. Some of them, according to legend, are said to come from Solomon's Temple. The pavement is in marble mosaic. The arches are decorated with mosaics depicting *Scenes from the Old and New Testaments*, most of which were made by Venetian craftsmen

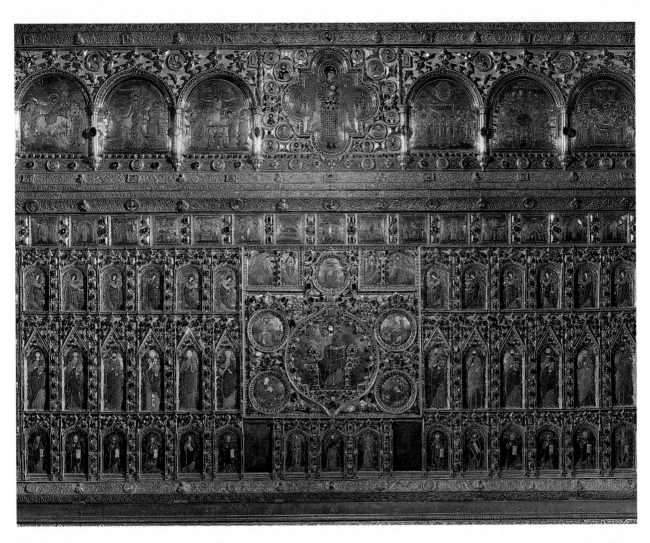

◄ *View of the rood screen in polychrome marble and the great Cross in gilded bronze made in 1393 by the Venetian goldsmith Jacopo di Marco Benato. On the left, the double ambo dating to the 14th century.*

The precious Pala d'Oro.

On the following pages, two pictures of the Pala d'Oro: detail of the center with Christ Enthroned blessing and the Four Evangelists, and the lower register with enamels, precious stones and the relief frame and the left part of the transept, with the rood screen and the Chapel of St. Peter.

after cartoons by Pietro Vecchia, Salviati, Titian and Pordenone.

The *tombs of Marino Morosini* (1253), *Bartolomeo Gradenigo* (1342) and *Felicita Falier* (1101) are also to be found in the atrium. A marble slab indicates the point where Frederick Barbarossa kneeled before Pope Alexander III on July 23, 1177.

The *interior* of San Marco is in the form of a Greek cross with five great hemispherical cupolas, one over each arm of the cross and one in the center. Galleries run along the interior of the church which is 76.50 meters long including the atrium and 62.60 m. wide at the transept. The central cupola is 43 meters high outside and 28.25 meters high inside.

In the left aisle at the end of the left transept is the **Chapel of the Madonna dei Mascoli** which belonged to a Confraternity of men only. The altar in flamboyant Gothic and dated 1430 is attributed to Giovanni Bon. The mosaics, variously attributed, fuse the old Venetian school with the Renaissance.

The **Altar of the Madonna Nicopeia** on the right aisle of the left transept preserves the famous image of the *Virgin of Victory*, a Byzantine painting with enamels which may date to the 10th century and which was brought to Venice from Constantinople in 1204 by Enrico Dandolo together with the famous bronze horses. Facing out onto the nave of the transept at the pier of the crossing is the **Altar of St. Paul**, an exquisite Renaissance creation.

21

The Sanctuary or Chancel is raised to allow for the crypt underneath, where the body of Saint Mark was once kept (now under the High Altar). The **Chapel of St. Peter**, to the left of the chancel, has statues by the Dalle Masegne brothers, a Gothic reliquary shrine, and *St. Andrew* and *St. Matthew* in mosaic on the underside of the arch overhead as well as a 13th-century mosaic of *St. Peter*.

Two doors behind the altar lead to the **Sacristy** and the small **Church of St. Theodore**. Some of the mosaics in the vault of the Sacristy are by Titian. The former church of St. Theodore was once the chapel of the Holy Office and has a splendid *Nativity*, an early work by G. B. Tiepolo, of 1732. Access to the apse is also from the Chapel of St. Peter. In the semidome of the apse is a 16th-century restoration of a mosaic of the *Blessing Christ*. Between the windows are the vestiges of the oldest mosaics in the Basilica which survived the fire of 1106.

View of the altar of the Sacrament in the central apse, showing the twisted alabaster columns and the door of the Ciborium by Sansovino.

View of the Chapel of the Madonna Nicopeia, with the altar of Tommaso Contino, 1617.

The Chapel of St. Isidore, in polychrome marble with the vault covered with 14th-century mosaics.

A mosaic in the Baptistery depicting the Dance of Salome (Venetian school — mid-14th century).

Treasury of San Marco: Icon of the Crucifixion (Byzantine art, 12th cent. ca.).

The *bronze doors* leading to the Sacristy are by Sansovino.

The *high altar* stands under a ciborium supported by four columns of oriental alabaster. The reliefs on the columns are by 13th-century Venetian artists. On top are the statues of the *Redeemer* and the *Evangelists*. On either side of the ciborium are four statues: the *Evangelists* by Jacopo Sansovino on the left, and the *Doctors of the Church* by Girolamo Paliari on the right.

Behind the altar is the famous scintillating **Gold Altar Screen**, the **Pala d'Oro**, a masterpiece of the goldsmith's art, 3.48 meters wide and 1.40 meters high. It was originally ordered by Doge Pietro Orseolo I (976-978) in Constantinople and was enriched in 1105 with gold and enamels brought from the Monastery of the Pantocrater at the time of the IV Crusade. It was later radically rearranged by Boninsegna. Some of the outstanding enamels include those depicting episodes from the *Life of Christ* and of *St. Mark* and the *Virgin*.

The cupola of the chancel is clothed with mosaics representing the *Religion of Christ foretold by the Prophets*. Separating the sanctuary from the body of the church is a marble iconostasis or rood screen, consisting of eight marble columns which support an architrave with fourteen statues. The mosaics in the great arch above represent scenes from the *Life of Christ* after car-

The famous Horses of the Basilica of San Marco.

Panorama of the domes of San Marco. ►

A view of the Piazzetta. ►

toons by Jacopo Tintoretto. The Doge and the high magistrates of the Republic took part in the religious functions from the sanctuary.

The **Chapel of St. Clement** has statues by the Dalle Masegne. From a small grated window, set to the right of the altar, the Doge could take part in the mass privately from the Ducal Palace.

The **Treaury of San Marco** is preceded by the Sanctuary in which 110 reliquaries and various religious paraphernalia are preserved. The Treasury proper contains the relics and precious objects that the Venetians have donated to the Republic throughout the centuries.

The **Baptistery** is called the Chiesa dei Putti (Church of the Babies) by the Venetians. It contains the funeral monument of Doge *Andrea Dandolo* and the sarcophagus of *Doge Giovanni Soranzo*. The *baptismal font* was designed in 1545 by Sansovino, whose mortal remains are

under the tombstone by the altar. In the cupolas and in the vaults are 14th-century mosaics of the Venetian school. The **Zen Chapel** is dedicated to Cardinal G. B. Zen who left a substantial legacy to the city when he died. On the bronze altar — in Lombardesque style — stands the *Madonna of the Shoe*, so-called because of a legend in which a poor man gave a shoe to the Madonna which was changed to gold. Thirteenth-century mosaics narrate episodes from the *Life of St. Mark*.

The entrance to the **Marciano Museum** or Museum of San Marco is next to the central door of the Church. The Museum is composed of a vast and precious collection of works of art, lace, carpets, and tapestries. The *organ doors* painted by Gentile Bellini are quite remarkable, as are the tapestries made to designs by Sansovino. The Museum also contains the *polyptych* by P. Veneziano which was formerly a case for the Pala d'Oro.

26

View from the top of the Palazzo Ducale or Palace of the Doges.

PALACE OF THE DOGES

The first Ducal Palace, or palace for the Doge, which could be more easily defended from enemy attacks via sea, could not have been built until at least a year or two after the government moved its headquarters from Malamocco to Venice at the beginning of the 9th century. In the second half of the 12th century Sebastiano Ziani, elected doge in 1172, decided to enlarge the original palace and the building took shape along the lines of its present ground plan.

Presumably this new building was more like a castle than a palace; in other words it was equipped with towers and defenses. In 1177 when Frederick Barbarossa came to Venice to be reconciled with Pope Alexander II he was a guest here. As the economic and commercial power of the State grew, the time came when the extant structures were no longer sufficient. In 1301 Doge Pietro Gradenigo decided to have a new palace built which would include a hall for the legislative assemblies and for the offices of the Chancellery.

With a decree of 1340 the construction of the Sala del Maggior Consiglio was established. Work began with the facade towards the lagoon and the first six arches on the Piazzetta. Chronicles report that the work was entrusted to Pietro Baseggio and his son-in-law Filippo Calendario.

The large spacious window overlooking the lagoon was commissioned by Doge Michele Steno from Jacobello and Pier Paolo Dalle Masegne in 1404, as witnessed by the date engraved at the top of the parapet. It is a beautiful example of flamboyant Gothic. The rest of the wing where the window was opened must have been built about forty years earlier, for in 1365 Guariento from Padua had been called in to fresco the upper hall with a *Paradise*. The difference between the wing on the waterfront and the old Ziani wing on the Piazzetta led the Venetian Senate to decide to demolish the latter and complete the whole palace in the style of the former. The construction was entrusted to Giovanni and Bartolomeo Bon and began on March 27, 1424 when Francesco Foscari was doge. Work was unquestionably terminated before 1457. In the same period (1438-1442) the so-called Porta della Carta, first known as « Grande » and then « Dorata », was built between the Palazzo and the Basilica.

In 1483 a raging fire destroyed the chapel, various rooms and the golden hall of the « Maps ». Antonio Rizzo from Verona was charged with the reconstruction and during the fifteen years he spent on the job he designed the *Scala dei Giganti*, the facades on the courtyard and towards the Rio di Palazzo. In April of 1498 however he was accused

28

of fraud and had to flee from Venice and the work was then entrusted to the « *proto* » (head architect) Pietro Solari known as Lombardo. Jacopo Sansovino finished the east wing between the Cortiletto dei Senatori (Senators' Courtyard), by the Basilica, and the original building overlooking the lagoon.

Another conflagration broke out on May 11, 1574, damaging the halls of the College and the Anticollege. Still another fire on December 10, 1577 ravaged the Halls of the Maggior Consiglio and the Scrutinio, destroying works by Bellini, Carpaccio, Veronese and Tintoretto. With Antonio Da Ponte in charge of rebuilding, the palace was restored to its original forms within the eight months promised.

Externally the upper part of the building is not nearly as airy as the lower part. From the Porta della Carta up to the Ponte della Paglia, the ground-floor portico with its pointed arches and columns without pedestals is echoed, on the floor above, by the long loggia with ogee arches and quadrilobate tracery. The upper floor, illuminated by large pointed-arch windows, is set above this loggia. The narrow crowning cornice is topped by airy oriental cresting. Openwork aedicules are on the corners.

After the fire of 1577, a statue of *Venice in the guise of Justice* by Alessandro Vittoria was set on the large window overlooking the waterfront. The niches at the sides have a figure of *St. Theodore*, and one of *St. George* by Antonio Canova. The window in the facade towards the Piazzetta was opened in 1537 after designs by Jacopo Sansovino. His pupils sculptured the statues of *Neptune* and *Mars* in the niches on either side. Above the balcony is a relief depicting *Doge Andrea Gritti kneeling before the winged Lion*, a copy by Ugo Bottasso of the original which was destroyed in the revolutionary uprisings of 1797. Crowning the window is a figure of *Justice* by Alessandro Vittoria (1579). Both the columns of the ground-floor portico and those of the loggia have sculptured capitals. The finest are those on the side facing the lagoon, since those on the Piazzetta are in part copies.

Particularly fine is the capital on the seventeenth column, counting from the corner at Ponte della Paglia, with the *Wise Men*, and also the seventh on the Piazzetta (starting at the waterfront) with *Marriage*, where the sculptor describes the life span of man and the marriage and domestic customs of the time in eight scenes, analytically describing the costumes worn by the Venetians in the 14th century.

There are also two scenes set one above the other at the corners of the facades. In the corner by the Ponte della Paglia the *Drunkenness of Noah* is below and the *Archangel Raphael and Tobias* are on the loggia at the corner of the Piazzetta on the waterfront, *Adam and Eve* are on the corner column and the *Archangel Michael* on the loggia. The corner towards the Basilica has the *Judgement of Solomon* below (attributed to Pietro Lamberti or Nanni di Bartolo) and above the Archangel Gabriel by Bartolomeo Bon.

The Porta della Carta and the Finestra Ducale.

◄ *A fascinating view of the courtyard of the Palace of the Doges.*

The Doges' Courtyard.

The **Porta della Carta** is one of the two main entrances to the palace. The other is the **Porta del Frumento** (Wheat Door) on the waterfront. A third entrance (the **Porta dell'Armar**) was opened on the Piazzetta in 1610. The name « della Carta » (of the paper) seems to derive from the fact that notices of the governmental decrees were posted here (or perhaps it was because the State Archives were nearby). The public scribes also seem to have had their stalls there. It is the work of Giovanni and Bartolomeo Bon, although what we see now is a radical 19th-century restoration, after the havoc wreaked in 1797. *Temperance* and *Fortitude* in the two lower niches are attributed to Antonio Rizzo. The figures of *Prudence* and *Charity*, in the upper niches, are also by the Bon family. Both the Porta della Carta and the Porta del Frumento give access to the **Courtyard** which is a finely balanced ensemble of works made over a range of 200 years, from

the 15th to the 17th century. There are two bronze *well-heads* in the center, by the master casters Alfonso Alberghetti (1559) (the one near the Foscari Porch) and by Nicolò Costi (1556) for the other. Right across from the entrance of the Porta della Carta (the so-called **Foscari Arch** begun by the Bons and completed by A. Rizzo and by Bregno) is the **Scala dei Giganti** or Giants' Staircase with the statues of *Mars* and *Neptune* by Sansovino. The coronation ceremony of the doge used to take place at the top of the Scala on a landing with arches, at the level of the first floor. After having sworn allegiance to the Most Serene Republic (« promissione ducale ») the doge was crowned by the oldest of the ducal Councilors. At the foot of the staircase, on the side facing the Basilica, is the **Cortiletto dei Senatori** where it is said the Senators assembled for particular ceremonies.

The east facade of the building was by Antonio Rizzo

31

The Doges' Courtyard: the Scala dei Giganti, or Giants' Staircase, a view of the colonnade of the gallery, one of the two well-heads and the Foscari Arch with the statue of Francesco I della Rovere, of 1587.

who began it after the fire of 1483. After his flight, the work was terminated by Pietro Lombardo. The part of the facade facing the Scala d'Oro was carried out by Scarpagnino (on designs by Rizzo). The **facades** to the south and west date to the early 17th century and were built under the direction of the *proto* Bartolomeo Manopola, eliminating the stables and the prisons. On the north side of the courtyard (also known as the Clock facade) there was once another staircase called the Scala Foscara or « del Piombo » because it was covered with lead plates. At the beginning of the 17th century it was demolished to make way for the new construction with the statue of the *Duke of Urbino* given to Venice by his nephew Francesco Maria della Rovere II.

The **loggia** on the first floor, which runs along three sides of the interior and two facades on the exterior, was built to provide access to all the offices of the various magistrates. An inscription by Vittoria on the loggia at the top of the Giants' Staircase refers to the visit the King of France, Henri III, made to Venice in 1574. Under the inscription is one of the many « lion's mouths » into which secret denunciations were inserted. The doorway to the right of the inscription leads to the **Hall of the lower Chancellory**, office of the « segretario alle voci » whose task it was to keep the registers of the offices and the

Two pictures of the Scala d'Oro or Golden Staircase.

The Room of the Four Doors: a detail of the ceiling and a ▶
view of the room. The painting on the left shows the Arrival
of Henry III in Venice.

proclamations for the elections. Then comes the **Stanza dei Provveditori alla Milizia da Mar**, a magistrature instituted in 1571 charged with raising an armed navy capable of defeating the Turks. As time passed their field of competence grew, eventually including the exacting of the « tithe », a tax of 10% on the wages of those in the pay of the Republic as well as of private individuals.

The **First Room** and the **Second Room of the Avogaria** were the offices of the Avogadori de Comun, fiscal lawyers comparable to a district attorney. They were also entrusted with the « Libro d'Oro » (Book of Gold) and the « Libro d'Argento » (Book of Silver), respectively listing the nobility and the bourgeoisie. Through a corridor it was possible to go from the second hall to the **Bridge of Sighs**, and from there to the **Prisons** which had two sections: the « piombi » and the » pozzi ». The latter (the wells) were situated at the level of the lagoon and were for those who had committed more serious crimes.

The **Scala d'Oro** or Golden Staircase, begun in 1583 on a design by Sansovino and completed by Scarpagnino in 1559, was a true ceremonial staircase used by the doge on his way to official ceremonies. Two doors open off the staircase which was reserved to illustrious personages and magistrates (one branch leads to the apartments of the doge). These doors lead to the **Sala degli Scudieri** (Pages' Room) and the **Sala del Magistrato al Criminal**.

The square drawing-room at the top of the Stairs contains works by J. Tintoretto (ceiling), Paolo Veronese and F. Bassano (on the walls). The left door leads to the **Cancelleria Ducale Superiore** and to the **Gran Cancelleria**, the one on the right to the **Room of the Four Doors** (delle Quattro Porte), a sort of antichamber for the **Anticollegio** and the **Collegio**. The former was used by those who were to be received by the doge in the « collegio », the latter was where the encounters of the doge with the Signoria della Serenissima, the Salvi Grandi and those of « Terraferma ed agli ordini » (comprising the full College) took place. It was where affairs of State were discussed.

The corridor next to the *throne* leads to the **Antichiesetta** (Antichapel), a sort of passageway to the **Secret Archives** and the **Ufficio del Savio Cassiere**. In the Chiesetta or Chapel the doge participated in mass every day, entering through the door to the right of the altar which communicates with stairs going down to the apartment on the floor below.

The **Andito del Consiglio dei Dieci** and the following **Sala del Consiglio** (Hall of the Council of Ten) are also reached from the Room of the Four Doors. Next in line is the so-called **Hall of the Bussola** which takes its name from the screened-off wooden box in the right corner. It is to all extents the interior of the « Bocca di Leone »

Two paintings in the Sala dell'Anticollegio: the Rape of Europa by Paolo Veronese and the Discovery of Arianne by Tintoretto.

◄ *View of the Sala dell'Anticollegio, or Waiting Room.*

◄ *The Lion of San Marco, painting by Vittore Carpaccio.*

37

Two pictures of the Sala del Collegio.

A view of the Sala del Senato and a detail of the ceiling with ►
the allegory of the League of Cambrais.

(Lion's Mouth) and was where the Fante dei Cai (the chief of Police) used to wait. The next room is that of the **Three Heads of the Consiglio dei Dieci**, chosen every month by the Council from its Ten members. The **Room of the State Inquisitors** is reached from here and then two corridors lead to the Prisons.

The corridor after the lefthand doorway of the Hall of the Bussola leads both to the **Hall of the Censors** and to the **Armeria** where what was salvaged from the destruction of 1797 has been collected in three halls (dedicated to Gattamelata, Morosini and Bragadin). The door at the back of the last hall leads to the doge's apartments consisting of various rooms. The doge's councilors waited in the **Sala degli Scarlatti** (named after the color of their robes). During his term of office, the arms of the prince were exhibited in the **Sala dello Scudo** or delle **Carte Geografiche**, and this is also where his bodyguards waited. The coat of arms now shown is that of the last doge, Ludovico Manin. The **Sala dei Filosofi** or Philosophers' Hall from which the doge had access to the stairs which led to the chapel owes its name to the twelve *Philosophers* painted by Veronese and Tintoretto, set in the walls be-

The Great Council Chamber.

The Sala della Quarantia Civil Vecchia and the Sala della ▶
Quarantia Criminale.

fore they were returned to the Libreria Vecchia (Sansovino Library). The **Sala degli Stucchi**, reached from the last door on the left, contains paintings by various masters, including Jacopo Tintoretto and G. B. Veneziano.

A door next to the fireplace (now walled up) led to the **Banquet Hall**. After the passage is the **Sala Erizzo**, a reception hall, followed by the **Sala Grimani** with a fine fireplace by the Lombardos.

Retracing one's steps and therefore recrossing the two rooms just described, we pass into the **Hall of the Quarantia Vecchia ai Civil** and the **Guariento Room** which was an arms deposit for the Maggior Consiglio. The remains of the *Paradise* painted by Guariento and damaged in the fire of 1577 are to be found here. The passage then leads to the **Sala del Maggior Consiglio**, or the Great Council Chamber, 54 m. long and 25 m. wide. All the nobles listed in the Libro d'oro who were over 25

years old automatically had the right to a seat, as well as thirty patricians between 25 and 30 years of age who were drawn by lot every year on the day of St. Barbara. An enormous canvas 7.65 m. by 24.6 m. dominates the back wall. Tintoretto painted it between 1588 and 1590 in the Scuola Vecchia della Misericordia. It has been restored more than once. Works by Veronese, Palma Giovane, A. Vicentini are also in the hall, on three sides of which runs a frieze with the *portraits of the doges*, two by two, painted by D. Tintoretto. Until 1902 many of the books of the Biblioteca Marciana were housed here.

The staircase that begins at the **Triumphal Arch** (honoring Doge Morosini, the Peloponnesiacus) leads down to the **Loggia Foscara** with a fine view of the Basilica, the Piazzetta, and the quay. This was where exhibitions were organized by the Congregations of Arts and Trades when the doge and dogaressa were crowned. The inner loggia

Three famous doges: Alvise Contarini, Marcantonio Trevisan and Marcantonio Bragadin.

(on the courtyard) then leads to the **Hall of the Censors**, a magistrature created in 1507 to keep an eye on possible election frauds. Access to the **Palazzo delle Prigioni** where the rooms have vaults in Istrian stone is from this room. A wooden staircase then leads to the « pozzi » or « wells » where the cells were marked with Roman numerals. The only cell that survived the destruction of 1797 is Roman numeral VII, still lined with wooden boards, a pallet in larch wood, and a small shelf.

The **Museo dell'Opera di Palazzo** on the ground floor has the original capitals from the exterior colonnade of the Doges' Palace (replaced during restoration), some columns, reliefs and original fragments from the crenellation and the architrave of the Porta della Carta.

DENONTIE SECRETE
CONTRO CHI OCCVLTERA
GRATIE ET OFFICII.
O COLLVDERA PER
NASCONDER LA VERA
RENDITA D ESSI.

The entrance corridor to the Prigioni Nuove.

The Lion's Mouth for anonymous accusations.

The interior of a cell in the prisons known as ''i Pozzi'', the ''Wells''.

The palace of the Doges seen from the Grand Canal.

The Drunkenness of Noah carved on the Doge's Palace at the corner of the Rio di Palazzo.

The famous Bridge of Sighs or Ponte dei Sospiri. ►

THE BRIDGE OF SIGHS

This small bridge over the Rio di Palazzo is one of the best-known monuments in the city and a must for the sight-seer. Its fame depends not so much on its architecture as it does on the 19th-century writers who often referred to it in their works and baptized it by this name. To tell the truth, in past centuries it must really have been a melancholy passage for those forced to cross it on their way from the prisons to the court or on their way back to the narrow dark cells of the Prigioni Nuove of the Most Serene Republic.

The prisons were built between the 16th and 17th centu-

The Palace of the Doges and the Ponte della Paglia.

The famous Venetian gondolas. ▶

ries on the other side of the Rio di Palazzo. Doge Marino Grimani then ordered the construction of a bridge to connect the place of confinement with the rooms of the Quarantia, the Tribunale and the Avogaria via two narrow superposed passageways. Built around 1602, possibly designed by Antonio Contin, the bridge is characterized by the exceptional height at which it is set and by the fact that it is completely covered, both overhead and at the sides. The edges of the arch are decorated with heads and over the span is a horizontal band articulated with rusticated pilaster strips and two small tracery windows in between. Further up a low-arched pediment with a relief of *Justice* seated between two lions is set under volutes.

The Ponte della Paglia and the Palace of the Prigioni Nuove.

Two views of the Riva degli Schiavoni. ▶

RIVA DEGLI SCHIAVONI

Ever since the 19th century when Napoleon had the Public Gardens installed near the eastern extremity, the Riva degli Schiavoni has been one of the typical promenades of the Venetians (and non-Venetians). Even before then the zone was buzzing with activity for as early as the 11th century this was where the boats moored, unloading and selling their merchandise here, work done mostly by sailors from Dalmatia (Schiavonia or Slav-land).

After the 14th-century **Ponte della Paglia**, near which the straw for the stables and the pallets of the prisoners of the Republic was unloaded, come the **Prigioni Nuove**, built between the 16th and 17th centuries and communicating with the back of the Palazzo Ducale via the Bridge of Sighs. Further on is the 15th-century **Palazzo Dandolo**, now Hotel Danieli, where kings and unforgettable figures

such as De Musset, Wagner, D'Annunzio, Dickens, and Balzac stayed. After the **Ponte del Vin** and the **Ponte della Pietà**, comes the **Church of the Pietà**, rebuilt between 1745 and 1760 by Massari and annexed to the **Hospital of the Pietà** or of the Esposti. The church houses prestigious works of sculpture and painting, including the *Coronation of the Virgin* by Giovanbattista Tiepolo, while the hostel, whose foundation, elsewhere, dates back to 1348, was the theater of Antonio Vivaldi's activity between 1703 and 1740.

Other monuments to be mentioned on the Riva degli Schiavoni include the former **Monastery of the Santo Sepolcro**, once a hostel for pilgrims on their way to the Holy Land and a monastery between 1745 and 1806, and the **Palazzo Gabrieli**, now a hotel, a 14th-century structure with a relief of the *Archangel Gabriel* on the facade and an elegant *well-head* in the courtyard.

GRAND CANAL

This long water-way (almost 4 kilometers) crosses just about all the city. Travelling along the canal is one way of seeing the highlights of Venice, for many of the most prestigious palaces line either side. The canal winds gently through the city, dividing it into two, connected by three bridges — the **Rialto**, the **Scalzi** and the **Accademia**.

Once upon a time the Grand Canal was the port of Venice, the point of arrival of trade for the flourishing Most Serene Republic. As time went by, the port gradually shifted and the Grand Canal became the « parlor » of Venice, a position it still holds today. From the 15th century on, the old houses in Byzantine style which lined the canal were replaced by prestigious palaces built along Gothic, Renaissance, or Baroque lines. These were golden centuries for Venice and this was also when various monumental churches went up along the Grand Canal, punctuating the procession of noble palaces. Churches such as the **Church of San Simeon Piccolo**, the **Church of the Scalzi**, with its monumental Baroque facade; the imposing **Church of San Geremia**, rebuilt in the 18th century; the 17th-century **Church of San Stae**, the **Church of San Samuele** dating back to the 11th century but rebuilt at the end of the 17th; the mighty **Church of Santa Maria della Salute**, one of the most interesting examples of Baroque architecture in Venice. But of equal interest from an architectural and stylistic point of view are the 17th-century **Palazzo Flangini**, the **Palazzo Querini** with its Gothic-Byzantine layout; the 17th-century **Palazzo Correr Contarini**, the 15th-century **Palazzo Giovanelli** with its striking Gothic structure, the elegant **Palazzo Vendramin-Calergi**, one of the finest Renaissance buildings in Venice and famous above all as the seat of the **Casinò Municipale**. Not to be overlooked are the unusual **Palazzo Belloni Battaglia** built in the same years as the Church of Santa Maria della Salute by the great architect Baldassarre Longhena; the spectacular scenographic **Fondaco dei Turchi** with its Venetian-Byzantine characteristics dating to the 12th and 13th centuries, seat of the **Museum of Natural History**; the **Ca' Corner della Regina** in 18th-century style, headquarters for the **Venice Biennale**; the **Ca' Pesaro**, remarkable example of Venetian Baroque and seat of the **Museums of Modern Art** and of **Oriental Art**; the sensual **Palazzo Sagredo**, Byzantine in origin but remodelled in the Gothic period; the 15th-century **Ca' d'Oro** with its ornate facade, housing the **Franchetti Gallery**. Next follows the **Fondaco dei Tedeschi**, an unusual example of 13th-century architecture, with the **Palazzo dei Camarlinghi** built in the 16th century along sober elegant lines; the **Palazzo Grimani**, one of the most interesting 16th-century buildings, and the sumptuous **Palazzo Papadopoli**, to continue with the 18th-century **Palazzo Grassi**, the **Palazzo Contarini degli Scrigni**, a fusion of two buildings of different periods (Renaissance, the one, Baroque the other), with the imposing **Palazzo Corner della Ca' Granda** built in the 16th century after plans by Sansovino and now housing the Prefettura. On the final stretch note should be taken of the exceptional **Palazzo Dario**, the most original example of 16th-century Venetian architecture, the **Palazzo Venier dei Leoni** with the **Peggy Guggenheim Collection**, and finally the **Doges' Palace**, rebuilt in the 12th century on 9th century foundations and then frequently restructured and enlarged in the ensuing centuries.

Palazzo Foscari-Contarini, dating to the first half of the 16th century.

Exterior of the church of San Simeon Piccolo, characterized by its great copper-green dome.

◄ *A view of the Grand Canal.*

CHURCH OF SAN SIMEON PICCOLO

The Church of San Simeon Piccolo overlooks the Grand Canal and almost reaches up to the edge of the water with the spacious entrance staircase. The building next to it is an example of mature 16th-century architecture, and housed the Scuola dei Tessitori di Panni di Lana (School for Woolen Cloth Weavers) whose patron saint was St. Simon. The original church, dedicated like this one, to the apostles St. Simon and St. Jude, was built in the 9th century. In 1718 it was torn down and replaced by the new church designed by Giovanni Scalfarotto on ideas by Longhena. Completed in 1738 the exterior is characterized by the greenish dome, sheathed in copper, with the figure of the *Redeemer* on top of the columned lantern. It is said that when Napoleon saw the building he remarked: « I have seen churches without domes, but never a dome without a church ». Apart from Napoleon's joking remark, the church really does look too small under the large dome, preceded by the spacious staircase and the tetrastyle porch which reduce the mass of the facade. The relief depicting the *Martyrdom of St. Simon and St. Jude* in the elegant pediment above the Corinthian columns is by Cabianca.

The **interior** with its circular ground plan is decorated with pilaster strips and columns, between which four altars open off. These are enriched by various works, as for instance *Saint Simon, Jude and John the Baptist* by Polazzo. Statues of the Apostles are in the apse near the high altar, which is decorated with 18th-century statues of *St. Simon and St. Matthew*. Of note also the marble *Crucifix* by Marchiari in the **Sacristy**.

*Santa Maria di Nazareth known also as the church
of the Scalzi when the Barefooted Carmelite Fathers took
it as their headquarters.*

CHURCH OF THE SCALZI

It took 35 years to finish the Church of the Scalzi or of
Santa Maria di Nazareth, begun in 1670, and commissioned from Baldassarre Longhena by the Barefooted
Carmelite Fathers for whom a convent and a small
church dedicated to Santa Maria di Nazareth had previ-
ously been built. The facade by G. Sardi successfully
combines the Venetian Baroque with classic forms. During World War I a fresco by Tiepolo, representing the
Transportation of the House of Loreto, was destroyed. It
has been replaced by a painting of the *Proclamation of
the Maternity of the Virgin at the Council of Ephesus*, by
Ettore Tito.

The **interior** has three chapels on either side of the nave.
The vault of the chapel on the right was painted by Tiepolo who also decorated the first chapel on the left. Ludovico Manin, the last doge of the Serenissima, is buried in
this church.

CHURCH OF SAN GEREMIA

San Geremia, near the Palazzo Labia, was restructured in
the 18th century on the old 13th-century church. The fine
Romanesque campanile in brick, one of the oldest in the
city, dates to the 1200s.

The Ponte degli Scalzi, built in stone in 1934 to replace the 19th-century bridge in iron.

The church of San Geremia.

PALAZZO VENDRAMIN-CALERGI

The loveliest palace in Lombardesque style is unquestionably the Palazzo Vendramin-Calergi at the Maddalena. Built between 1504 and 1509 by the Lombardos on designs by Mauro Codussi, two floors of loggias with large arches and two-light openings characterize the large finely proportioned facade. In the 17th century a wing with garden, designed by the architect Scamozzi, was added, only to be torn down later and then rebuilt from scratch. It was in this palace that Richard Wagner died in 1883.

Casa Gatti-Casazza, a reconstruction in 18th-century style, next to the church of San Marcuola.

The Renaissance facade of the Palazzo Vendramin-Calergi, seat of the Casino Municipale.

The church of San Marcuola serves as backdrop for the Campo dei SS. Ermagora e Fortunato. The facade is incomplete but preserves the portal of the original 18th-century project by Giorgio Massari. Actually tradition sets the foundation of the church in the 9th century. Remodelled in the 17th century, it was definitively transformed by Gaspari, but he had not yet terminated work in 1728 and it was carried out by Massari in 1736, except for the facade.

FONDACO DEI TURCHI

The Fondaco dei Turchi is one of the first warehouses to have been founded in Venice. The basic layout, in fact, dates to the 12th-13th centuries, and is Veneto-Byzantine in style. It was acquired in 1381 by the Republic who turned it over to the dukes of Ferrara. It then belonged to various wealthy families and ended up by becoming the warehouse and headquarters of the Turkish community between 1621 and 1838. It was originally of such beauty that the Serenissima used it as a guest house for important personages. Even so the exterior is now quite different from what it looked like originally: between 1858 and 1869 Berchet restored and altering it.

CA' PESARO

The Palazzo Pesaro is by Baldassarre Longhena, one of the greatest architects of the 17th century. It was begun in 1652 and finished by Antonio Gaspari. The facade is decorated with masks and various ornaments with busts of animals.

The Fondaco dei Turchi.

Ca' Pesaro with the Rio di Noale in the background.

Palazzo di Ca' Pesaro, seat of the Museum of Modern Art. ►

Palazzo Gussoni, subsequently Gussoni Grimani ''della Vida'', ►

The Ca' d'Oro is the most perfect example of flamboyant Gothic architecture in Venice: below, a detail of the facade.

A fine picture of the palaces that border the left bank of the ►
Grand Canal. To the left of the Ca' d'Oro, the Palazzo Miani
Coletti Giusti and the 17th-century Palazzo Fontana
Rezzonico. To the right of the Ca' d'Oro is the Palazzo Pesaro.

Palazzo Pesaro, in 15th-century Venetian Gothic style, with ►
the adjacent facade of Palazzo Morosini-Sagredo. The latter
originally dates to the Byzantine period (13th cent.) but it was
remodelled in later centuries.

CA' D'ORO

The famous Ca' d'Oro, far and away the finest example of flamboyant Gothic, houses the **Franchetti Gallery**. The palace was built for Marino Contarini between 1424 and 1430 by Giovanni and Bartolomeo Bon. The name derives from the marble tracery and the gilding which once decorated the facade. In 1846 Giovanni Battista Meduna began restoration but removed and sold the original facing, for which he was brought to court. After changing hands many times, the palace finally came into the possession of Baron Giorgio Franchetti who restored it completely before donating the palace and the works it contained to the city in 1915. The ashes of the baron repose under a column in the palace courtyard.

PALAZZO SAGREDO

The late 14th-century Palazzo Sagredo — now Istituto Ravà — is near the Ca' d'Oro. There is an elegant four-light opening on the upper floor surrounded by a Venetian-Byzantine frieze, and a fine six-light opening on the lower floor.

The Grand Canal with some of its palaces: Michiel delle Colonne, Michiel dal Brusà and Smith Mangilli Valmarana, which also look out on the Rìo dei SS. Apostoli. ►

Rio delle Beccarie and the Pescaria. ►

Still another picture of the lovely Palazzo Sagredo.

Campo di Santa Sofia and the small Palazzo Foscari del Prà, erected in the second half of the 15th century. The ambassador of Mantua lived here in 1520.

PESCARIA

The statue of *St. Peter* decorates the arcading of the Pescaria on the side which overlooks the Grand Canal. The neo-Gothic forms were designed in 1907 by Rupolo and Laurenti, who skillfully harmonized them with the neighboring structures. This was once the site of the 13th-century house of the Querini who took part in the conspiracy of Bajamonte Tiepolo and who then had their house confiscated and almost totally destroyed, with the exception of a few arches and a two-light opening towards the Campo delle Beccarie. This large portico is now the headquarters of the fish market, facing out on the Grand Canal and the Rio delle Beccarie to facilitate restocking, not far from the Cordaria, the Erbaria and the Casaria, where fruit and cheese are sold.

A picture of the Pescaria and, in the photo below, a panorama of Venetian palaces: Palazzo Michiel delle Colonne, Palazzo Michiel de Brusà and Palazzo Mangilli-Valmarana. The name of the second palace clearly refers to the fire (brusa = scorch or burn) which gutted it in 1774. The last-named palace was the abode of the English consul Joseph Smith, a passionate collector of art and patron of artists including Rosalba Carriera, the Ricci and above all Canaletto. His collection included about 50 canvases and over 140 drawings by Canaletto and in 1760 he left them all to the English Crown.

FONDACO DEI TEDESCHI

Next to the eastern end of the Ponte di Rialto is the Fondaco (or in Venetian dialect, Fontego) dei Tedeschi, a magnificent early 16th-century building. This large warehouse and clustering of shops already existed in the 13th century, but it was wiped out by a fire and then rebuilt in its present forms. Even so the facade on the Grand Canal is no longer just as Girolamo Tedesco designed it, for the two towers at the corners were demolished in the 19th century. The original structure, built by the architects Spavento and Scarpagnino between 1505 and 1508 had also been covered with magnificent frescoes by Giorgione and Titian. Time has cancelled almost all traces.

In the headquarters for the German merchants in Venice — a numerous colony which played an important role in the economy of the city, now is the post office.

Palazzo Ca' da Mosto, built between the 11th and 13th century. From the 16th to the 18th century the palace became the ''Albergo del Leon Bianco'', one of the best and most important hotels in Venice.

The twenty-five arches of the Fabbriche Nuove di Rialto, possibly built on designs by Jacopo Sansovino between 1552 and 1555.

The Fondaco dei Tedeschi. ►

On the following pages: the Ponte di Rialto.

Two pictures of the famous Ponte di Rialto: the cost of rebuilding it in stone, on a project by Antonio da Ponte, cost all of 250,000 ducats in 1590. The single span is notched into the fondamenta.

PONTE DI RIALTO

The first Rialto Bridge was called « della Moneta ». The original pontoon bridge was erected by Nicolo Barattieri and the wooden structure which replaced it was destroyed during the uprisings in the plot of Bajamonte Tiepolo. The next bridge collapsed in 1444 and was replaced by one which included a drawbridge and shops. When this also showed signs of instability, it was rebuilt in stone, preference being given to the design by Antonio Ponte, rather than to those of famous architects such as Michelangelo, Sansovino, and Palladio. The bridge (finished in 1592) has a single span of 28 meters (at the point where the Grand Canal is narrowest) and is 7.5 meters above the water-line.

PALAZZO PAPADOPOLI

The Renaissance Palazzo Papadopoli is a two-story building attributed to Gian Giacomo dei Grigi. Of particular note the fine cornice with small oval windows and two obelisks above. Inside are to be found paintings by Tiepolo and Pietro Longhi.

PALAZZO BERNARDO

Palazzo Bernardo must be cited as one of the best examples of Gothic style, both on account of its sumptuous ornament and the harmonious forms, where voids and solids are perfectly balanced. Built in 1442, there are two six-light windows on the first two floors, each surmounted by a four-light opening.

Above: the facades of the Papadopoli and Bernardo palaces. Below: a picture of the Grand Canal with Palazzo Papadopoli, Palazzo Businello (built in the 17th century on a preexisting Byzantine structure) and the contiguous Palazzo Lanfranchi. ▶

A view of the Ponte di Rialto and the Riva del Ferro.

At the center of the picture Palazzo Corner Loredan and the Ca' Farsetti, separated by a narrow calle, house the Town Hall.

Three of the most prestigious Venetian palaces which overlook the Grand Canal: Palazzo Foscari, Palazzo Balbi and Palazzo Nani-Mocenigo.

◄ Palazzo Giustinian Persico stands at the corner between the Grand Canal and the Rio di San Tomà.

CA' FOSCARI

An outstanding example of flamboyant Gothic is Ca' Foscari, one of the loveliest buildings in Venice. The facade is richly decorated in marble with two superposed loggias of eight arches each, surrounded by windows which repeat the decorative motive. The whole is crowned by an imposing motive of arches, with a central four-light opening at the uppermost floor. The palace originally belonged to the Giustinian family, was acquired by the Republic, and given first to the Duke of Mantua and then to Francesco Sforza. It was auctioned off in 1452 and became the property of Doge Foscari.

PALAZZO BALBI

Palazzo Balbi, facing onto the canal (« in volta di canal »), built at the end of the 16th century after a design by Alessandro Vittoria, in a sense seems to mark the transition between the sober spatial proportions of the Renaissance and the heavy decoration of the Baroque.

PALAZZO NANI-MOCENIGO

Palazzo Nani-Mocenigo, formerly Erizzo, stands on the left bank of the Grand Canal. Built in the 15th century, it is characterized by the first- floor windows with dentellated surrounds framing carenate arches.

PALAZZO GRASSI

This imposing building, by the architect Giorgio Massari, is one of the finest examples of 18th-century architecture. On either side of the tall portal, Palazzo Grassi has two tiers of windows, set into the rustication, above which are two other tiers of balconied windows. It now houses the Centro delle Arti e del Costume and is the permanent headquarters for all kinds of cultural activities.

CA' REZZONICO

Palazzo Rezzonico was begun by Longhena and terminated in 1745 by Giorgio Massari. It is a typical example of 18th-century architecture and quite suitably houses the Museum of the Eighteenth Century (Museo del Settecento). The building stretches out along the Grand Canal and the facade, enlivened by balconies, is ornamented with columns and sculpture.

PALAZZI GIUSTINIAN

Various palaces go by the name of the powerful Giustinian family, from the one at the Traghetto di Calle Vellaresso, dating to 1474 — headquarters of the offices of the Biennale — to the one near Ca' Foscari which consists of twin buildings with loggias of quadrilobate arches and was where Wagner also lived.

PONTE DELL'ACCADEMIA

The southernmost crossing on the Grand Canal is the Accademia Bridge whose broad wooden span connects Campo San Vidal to Campo della Carità with the Scuola Grande di Santa Maria della Carità, now the site of the Galleria dell'Accademia. The origins of this footbridge are not as old as the use of wood, typical for the 14th-century Venetian bridges, would lead one to believe. It is a modern (1934) structure, by Miozzi, and was erected as a temporary replacement for the metal bridge which had been built in 1854 and was soon criticized as being excessively « modern ». The same thing happened for the Ponte degli Scalzi. Plans were therefore made for a stone bridge, closer in style to the adjacent buildings, so that the historical Ponte di Rialto would be flanked by two other bridges in Istrian stone at the Scalzi and at the Accademia. Only the former however was actually built in that year — 1934 — and a temporary structure went up for the latter. Eventually this was accepted as definitive, despite the fact that today the material of which it is made clearly betrays the passage of time.

Palazzo Grassi.

Ca' Rezzonico.

Palazzo Giustinian Lolin, an early work by Baldassarre Longhena, with the two pinnacles decorating the roof, and the 16th-century Palazzo Civran Badoer Barozzi. ►

The Ponte dell'Accademia and the Palazzo Cavalli Franchetti, where the archduke Frederick of Austria died in 1836. ►

The Grand Canal with, left to right, the Palazzo Cavalli Franchetti and the Palazzo Barbaro now Curtis, separated by the Rio dell'Orso. In the background on the right, the church of Santa Maria della Salute.

Above: on the left the Palazzo Brandolini Rota (in which the ▶ poet Robert Browning lived in 1878) and the back of the Ponte dell'Accademia; on the right the front view of the Galleria dell'Accademia (Giogio Massari and Bernardino Maccarucci, 1756-65). Below: on the left the Palazzo Corner della Ca' Granda, so-called for its majestic proportions; on the right the Palazzo Minotto, originally Byzantine and rebuilt in Gothic style during the 15th century.

PALAZZO BARBARO

Near the Ponte dell'Accademia, on the left of the Grand Canal is the Palazzo Barbaro (15th cent.) with four-light windows with carenate arches on the upper floors and a fine Renaissance portal with medallions of the emperors.

SCUOLA GRANDE DI SANTA MARIA DELLA CARITÀ

The Scuola Grande di Santa Maria della Carità was founded in 1260 at San Leonardo but was then transferred, first to the Oratory of San Giacomo Apostolo, and then to an Oratory of its own near the Church of Santa Maria della Carità. A *Madonna with Confraternity Brothers* is set over the portal with the Confraternity patron saints, *Christopher and Leonardo*, on either side. The large room on the ground floor is divided into two parts, one serving as entrance to the **Gallerie dell'Accade-** mia and the other as the hall of the **Accademia delle Belle Arti**. Works originally in the guest-room include a reliquary donated in 1463 by Cardinal Bessarione, the *Presentation of the Virgin*, painted for the Confraternity by Titian, and the large *Triptych* by Antonio Vivarini and Giovanni d'Alemagna of the *Virgin and Child with the Doctors of the Church*, as well as works by Bellini, G. Mansueti, G. Cignaroli, J. Guarana, G. D. Tiepolo, and Marieschi.

CA' GRANDA

Palazzo Corner, known as Ca' Granda, is one of the most imposing examples of Renaissance architecture. By Jacopo Sansovino (1537), it is the seat of the Prefecture. The facade is divided into three stories — rusticated, Ionic and Corinthian, with three arches on the ground floor and large round-headed arches on the windows. Of note, inside, a majestic courtyard with a statue of *Apollo* by Cabianca.

A view of Palazzo Barbaro (left) and Palazzo Dario (right). The first was built in Gothic style in the middle of the 15th century. The second with its strongly tilted silhouette, was built in 1478 for Giovanni Dario, secretary of the Republic in Constantinople. The originally Gothic building has a Renaissance facade by Pietro Lombardo, characterized by polychrome marble inlays which form medallions and plates.

Palazzo Venier dei Leoni: the building which overlooks the Grand Canal is only the ground floor of what, as initially planned, was to have been a palace as imposing as the Corner della Ca' Granda across the way. The palace, begun in 1749 by Boschetti but never finished for lack of funds, owes its name to the fact that noble Venier family used to keep one or more lions in the garden. It was bought by the famous American art collector Peggy Guggenheim, and today is the seat of one the most prestigious collections of contemporary art: from Bacon to Picasso, from Braque to Kandinsky, from Ernst to Dali, etc.

Palazzo Barbarigo, 16th century, stands at the corner between ▶ the Grand Canal and the Campo San Lio: the mosaics that decorate the facade in parallel bands are 19th-century and were taken from cartoons by Giulio Carlini.

A picture of the Grand Canal with a gondola — the classic ▶ Venetian boat — and, on the right, the Palazzo Pisani Gritti.

GUGGENHEIM COLLECTION

The most important Italian collection of contemporary art is without the shadow of a doubt the Guggenheim Collection, housed in the **Palazzo Venir dei Leoni** on the Grand Canal, a building begun in 1749 on designs by Lorenzo Boschetti. It was never completed and is surrounded by a fine garden. The works of art on exhibit furnish a complete picture of the avant-garde artistic movements of the 20th century, from Cubism, with paintings by Picasso — *The Poet, Lacerba* —, Duchamp — *Sad Young Man in a Train* —, Braque, Kupka, Marcoussis, to Futurism with works by Boccioni, E. Prampolini, G. Severini. Abstract art is represented by Kan-

dinsky, Mondrian — *The Sea* —, Malevich — with *Suprematist Composition*, while particular attention is paid to Dadaism and Surrealism (particularly in view of the ties between Peggy Guggenheim and Max Ernst, a painter whose place in the historical avant-garde is ensured), with works by De Chirico, Ernst — of his many paintings mention is made of *The Kiss, The Forest, Zoomorphic Couple* —, Magritte, Paul Klee, Picabia and Mirò. The collection includes examples of the more recent avant-garde movements as well, both European and American, with works by Moore, Pollock and Arnaldo Pomodoro.

◄ *Above, left to right: the Palazzo Contarini-Fasan with its lovely balusters in openwork marble on the terraces and the Palazzo Contarini in Gothic style and dating to the 15th century. Below: the last stretch of the Grand Canal in the vicinity of the Piazzetta San Marco. On the left is the Palazzo Giustinian — a 15th-century building — at present headquarters for the offices of the Biennale, and a series of unimposing buildings.*

The domes of the church of Santa Maria della Salute and the Punta della Dogana.

PALAZZO CONTARINI-FASAN

The delightful small Contarini-Fasan palace, built around 1475 and popularly known as the « house of Desdemona », stands on the left bank of the Grand Canal, near the Rio delle Ostreghe, and is decorated with charming tracery balconies.

CHURCH OF SANTA MARIA DELLA SALUTE

In 1630 with the plague raging in Venice, the Senate made a vow to erect a church to the Madonna when the scourge came to an end. In fulfillment of this obligation Baldassarre Longhena designed Santa Maria della Salute, which was consecrated in 1687, five years after the architect's death. The church is unquestionably one of the great monuments of the Venetian Baroque.

The building is octagonal in plan with arches dominated by a dome on a drum and with six side chapels. A flight of stairs leads to the **facade** which looks like a rich triumphal arch, with chapels set into the sides of the octagon. The first three altars on the right in the **interior** have paintings by Luca Giordano and the third altar on the left has a late work by Titian of the *Pentecost*. Around 1674 Giusto Le Court created the marble group on the high altar, meant to house the Holy Image that was venerated in San Tito in Candia and then brought to Venice in 1672 when the Turks occupied the city. The sculpture shows us the *Plague fleeing from the Madonna*. Originally the commission was to have been given to Bernini, but he refused. Canvases by Titian are in the ceiling of the large Sacristy and the tabernacle has a fine mosaic in pietre dure of the Byzantine school of the 12th century. The Venetians flock to the church in pilgrimage on the 21st of November, the day dedicated to the Madonna della Salute.

◄ *The Palazzo Genovese, of 1892, and the church of Santa Maria of the Salute.*

Aerial view of the Punta della Dogana dominated by the church of Santa Maria della Salute.

DOGANA DA MAR

The complex of the Maritime Customs House, at the far end of the sestiere (district) of Dorsoduro, is a sort of spearhead jutting out into the lagoon and dividing the Grand Canal from the Canal of the Giudecca. Behind it, beyond the Seminary, Santa Maria della Salute looms up. At the beginning of the 15th century, the area whose elegant layout we now admire was already used for the docking of ships from the Orient and their clearance by customs. The sheds built to house the merchandise and the customs officials were rebuilt more than once. The construction of the **Punta della Dogana** with a tower which rises up over the terraced porch dates to 1677. Set on a base on the roof of the tower are figures of two slaves holding up a large gilded sphere on which the statue of *Fortune* (a 17th-century work by Giuseppe Bononi) stands on one foot, free to turn with the wind, as changeable as human destinies at the mercy of the seas and trade.

The arcaded structures along the sides date, as can be seen, to different periods. Parts are in stone with light-colored arched openings and parts are completely faced in white on more serried rows of arches. The latest renovation was carried out by Pigazzi, in 1838.

CHURCH OF THE SANTI APOSTOLI

The extremely old church of the Santi Apostoli was frequently remodelled up to 1575 when it was radically renovated. In the 18th century Giuseppe Pedola once more changed its form. The **facade** is in brick. **Inside** — a single rectangular nave — the **Corner Chapel** contains the *Tomb of Marco Corner*, attributed to Tulio Lombardo. The altarpiece with the *Communion of St. Lucy* is by G. B. Tiepolo.

CHURCH OF SANTA MARIA DEI MIRACOLI

In 1481 Pietro Lombardo began the construction of Santa Maria dei Miracoli in Lombard style. The **facade** with its marble facing in two tiers is particularly striking. Two large windows are set above the central portal. The walls of the single-nave **interior** are faced with fine marble and the barrel-vaulted ceiling is decorated with coffering containing the heads of *Prophets and Saints* by Pier Maria Pennacchi.

The sanctuary has an elegant staircase with statues of *St. Francis*, *St. Claire*, the *Virgin of the Annunciation and Gabriel*, by Tullio Lombardo. The high altar is crowned by a dome.

The church of the Santi Apostoli.

The original facade of the church of Santa Maria dei Miracoli.

A shot of the famous Historical Regatta.

THE HISTORICAL REGATTA

One of the festivals in Venice which is still in full force is the Historical Regatta, providing entertainment for the Venetians and all those who come from near and far to see the colorful event. Many doubts exist as to when the first regatta was held and why, but we do know that in the 13th-14th centuries the race had become customary. As is still the case today, the race itself was preceded by a sumptuous procession of all kinds of boats, all decked out and bearing symbolic images. The finest of all was the **Bucintoro**, the doge's ceremonial barge, now replaced by a smaller version. An idea of what the original gilded galley looked like is provided by various paintings and the model in the Naval Museum. After the parade, which was once a real *défilé* for the nobility, the races began. Originally the boats were divided into categories according to the number of rowers (once even twenty or fifty), but now there are only two per boat. The route to be covered in the least possible time goes from the Motta to Castello and Santa Chiara on the Grand Canal and back to the Ca' Foscari where a floating pavilion (*machina*) marks the finish line. The winning team is awarded with a banner while a piglet is jokingly « conferred » on the loser.

The 17th-century facade of the church of San Moisè.

CHURCH OF SAN ZACCARIA

The original Church of San Zaccaria dates to the 9th century but it was rebuilt after the fire of 1105 and transformed in Gothic style between the 15th and 16th centuries by Antonio Gambello and Mauro Codussi. The extremely tall **facade** has a large arched pediment as its crowning element with a row of blind niches and decorative panels. The lovely statue of *St. Zaccariah* over the portal is by Alessandro Vittoria.

The **interior** (with tall columns dividing the two side aisles from the nave in a perfect fusion of Gothic and Renaissance styles) contains an *altarpiece* by Giovanni Bellini, a *Madonna and Saints* by Palma Vecchio, the *Birth of the Baptist* by Tintoretto and the *Flight to Egypt* by G. D. Tiepolo. *Frescoes* by Andrea del Castagno are to be seen in the **San Tarasio Chapel**, as well as three *polyptychs* by Giovanni d'Alemagna and Antonio Vivarini. The sepulcher of A. Vittorio, with his self-portrait, is at the back of the left aisle. The two holy water fonts in the church as well as the statues of the *Baptist* and of *St. Zaccariah* near the entrance are by Vittoria. In his testament he also donated his house in Calle della Pietà to the nuns of San Zaccaria and asked to be buried in the church.

San Zaccaria, interior: the famous altarpiece by Bellini. ▶

The facade of the Church of San Zaccaria.

CHURCH OF SAN MOISÈ

The original 8th-century church was rebuilt in the 10th century for a certain Moisè Venier who wanted it dedicated to his patron saint. In the 14th century a campanile in brick with two-light openings in the belfry was added. The facade, which is particularly lovely, with a wealth of sculpture, is the work of Alessandro Tremignon and the sculptor Enrico Meyring and dates to the second half of the 17th century.

The church with its single nave contains many 17th- and 18th-century paintings. Carved wooden *choir stalls* dating to the 16th century are in the sanctuary. In the chapel on the left are a *Last Supper* by Palma Giovane and a *Washing of the Feet* by Jacopo Tintoretto.

Aerial view of the church of Santi Giovanni e Paolo.

The church of Santi Giovanni e Paolo, the monument to ▶
Colleoni and the Scuola Grande di San Marco.

CHURCH OF SANTI GIOVANNI E PAOLO (SAN ZANIPOLO)

The construction of the church of Santi Giovanni e Paolo or San Zanipolo was begun in 1246, but it was not till 200 years later, in 1430, that the building could be termed finished. It is, without doubt, a stupendous example of Venetian Gothic. The church was used for the funerals of the doges and every year, on June 26th, was visited by the doge and the high officials.

The mortal remains of various doges and condottieri lie within the church, including Jacopo and Lorenzo Tiepolo, Daniele Boni. Nor should one overlook the *Mausoleum to the Valier Family* by Andrea Tirali, the various *monuments of the Mocenigo and Valier families*, as well as the *Monument to Bartolomeo Bragadin* in Lombardesque style and the one to *Marcantonio Bragadin* by Scamozzi. And then the *Tomb of Vettor Pisani*, the *Monument to Doge Marco Corner*, in Gothic style.

Artists such as Giovanni Bellini, Piazzetta, Lorenzo Lotto, B. Vivarini, Palma Giovane and Nino Pisano worked in the church.

Next door is the **Scuola Grande di San Marco**, originally dating to 1260 but then rebuilt, after a fire, by Pietro Lombardo and Mauro Codussi between 1485 and 1495.

EQUESTRIAN MONUMENT TO BARTOLOMEO COLLEONI

The equestrian statue of Bartolomeo Colleoni looms up on a high pedestal in the Campo dei Santi Giovanni e Paolo, in front of the Scuola Grande di San Marco. This mercenary captain was involved in various exploits on the side of the Serenissima in the war against Filippo Maria Visconti in 1431, helping to counterbalance the negative trend of the campaigns undertaken by Carmagnola. When hostilities with the Visconti were resumed, Colleoni — together with Gattamelata — was once more in the ranks of the Venetians (1437-41). After a period passed in the hire of the adversaries, in 1448 he returned to the Serenissima together with Sforza, responsible for the victories of Caravaggio, Sciesa, Borgomanero and the campaigns in the countryside around Brescia, Bergamo and Parma. After having passed to the other side for the last time, he finally became head of the Venetian troops from 1454 to 1457, the year of his death which found him in the pomp of his castle in Malpaga.

When he died he left most of his considerable patrimony to the Republic, on the condition that a statue to him be erected in Piazza San Marco. Since by law no monument could be raised there, his statue was placed in Campo San Zanipolo.

Andrea Verrocchio worked on the statue between 1481 and 1488 but died before casting it in bronze, a job which, together with the finishing touches, was entrusted

to Alessandro Leopardi, who inaugurated the statue in 1496 after also having designed the high base with columns and panels.

SCUOLA GRANDE DI SAN MARCO

The phenomenon of the institution of the so-called schools which characterized the Italian Middle Ages was also evident in Venice with congregations and associations whose prime purpose was mutual assistence and works of charity.
« Scuole » or « Schools » were thus constituted, of greater or lesser importance depending on the number of brethren involved.
The six Schools known as « Grandi » were solely devotional in character.
The Scuola Grande di San Marco founded in 1260 was once in the edifice which now houses the Ospedale Civile or Hospital. Destroyed by fire, it was rebuilt by Mauro Codussi and Pietro Lombardo between 1485 and 1495.
The **facade** is a fine example of Renaissance architecture. The statues are by B. Bon and Tullio Lombardo. On the first floor the **Chapter Hall** has a 16th-century wooden *ceiling* and an *altar* by the school of Sansovino. In the Hostel Hall (**Sala dell'Albergo**) there is another lovely ceiling with decorations in gold and blue, by Pietro and Biagio Faenza. On the walls are paintings by Palma Giovane, Mansueti and Vittore Belliniano. The hall also contains the **Medical Library**. The cycle with the *Stories of Saint Mark*, by Carpaccio, the Bellinis, and Tintoretto, some of which are now in the Galleria dell'Accademia, were originally on the floor above.

Two views of the characteristic Rio Santa Maria Formosa and picture of the church.

CHURCH OF SANTA MARIA FORMOSA

The original church of Santa Maria Formosa which seems to have been built in the 7th century was renovated time and time again. The present edifice is by Codussi. The two **facades** date to different periods (the one facing the bridge to 1541 and the one on the Campo to 1604). The **bell tower** is Baroque with a double balcony on either side of the belfry and an interesting grotesque mask over the entrance doorway.

The Latin-cross interior has a nave only. A splendid *triptych* by Bartolomeo Vivarini is in a chapel on the right, while a polyptych with *St. Barbara and Four Saints* by Palma Vecchio is in the right transept. Take note of the *altar of the Scuola dei Bombardieri* which had its home in this church and in which a small bombard is preserved.

Two pictures of the Rio San Giovanni Nuovo.

The picturesque Rio del Vin.

The distinguished Rio Palazzo. ▶

CHURCH OF SAN GIACOMO DELL'ORIO

In 1225 the Church of San Giacomo dell'Orio was rebuilt on the site of an earlier 9th-century church and was then renovated in the 16th century. To one side is the fine brick **campanile** with a four-light opening in the belfry. In the Latin-cross interior different styles fuse together while a wooden carinate vault covers both sanctuary and crossing. The numerous works of art include an *altarpiece* by Veronese, panel paintings by Buonconsiglio and Schiavone, and, in the **Old Sacristy**, a cycle of paintings by Palma Giovane with scenes from the *Old Testament*.

◄ *The Fondamenta Papafava and the Ponte Malvasia.*

Above: the church of San Giacomo dell'Orio, in the Campo of the same name and the Rio near the church. Below: Calle del Tentor and Rio in Santa Croce.

The bell tower of San Giovanni Elemosinario and Campo San Polo, with the bell tower of the church of San Polo.

◄ Fondamenta Rio Marin and Campo Nazario Sauro.

CHURCH OF SAN GIOVANNI ELEMOSINARIO

First built in the 11th century, San Giovanni Elemosinario was destroyed by fire in 1513 and rebuilt by Scarpagnino in the same century. It is a Greek cross in plan. The ceiling and the altar in the sacristy have works by G. B. Pittoni while a fine *Saint John Elemosinario* by Titian is on the high altar in the sanctuary and works by Pordenone and Palma Giovane are to be found in the side chapels.

Of note the small brick **campanile**, with fine arches in the belfry, which survived the fire of 1513 intact.

CHURCH OF SAN POLO

Apparently San Polo was founded by Doge Pietro Gradenigo. It was rebuilt in Gothic style and then frequently remodelled. The brick **campanile** with a conic steeple dates to 1361. The **interior** is a basilica with a nave and two aisles. It contains works by Jacopo Tintoretto, Palma Giovane, G. B. Tiepolo and Alessandro Vittoria.

SCUOLA GRANDE
DI SAN GIOVANNI EVANGELISTA

The Scuola Grande di San Giovanni Evangelista, one of the oldest of the Venetian Scuole or Guilds was housed in a hospice founded in 1261. The Gothic **facade**, which contains two 14th-century *reliefs*, dates to 1454. In the courtyard of the Scuola there is a fine *doorway* built in 1512 after plans by Mauro Codussi. On the ground floor the **interior** has a Renaissance hall by Codussi. On the walls are canvases by Longhi and Vicentino while the *ceiling* is decorated with *scenes from the Apocalypse* by Guarana and Tiepolo. Paintings by Palma Giovane and stucco decorations are in the **Oratorio della Croce** and the **Sala dei Convocati**.

CHURCH OF SAN GIACOMO DI RIALTO

The Church of San Giacomo di Rialto, traditionally the oldest church in Venice, is in the Ruga degli Orefici. Dating back to the 11th century, it was completely restored in the 17th century. On the facade over the fine 15th-century portico is a large distinctive *clock*, also 15th-century, and a small Gothic tabernacle with a charming statue of a *Madonna and Child*.

Rio San Silvestro and a rio in the sestiere San Polo. ▶

Campiello della Scuola Grande di San Giovanni Evangelista and the church of San Giacomo di Rialto.

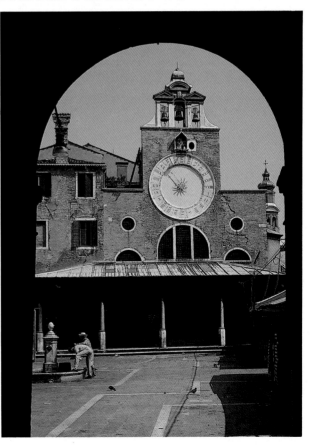

CHURCH OF SANTA MARIA GLORIOSA DEI FRARI

Santa Maria Gloriosa dei Frari, a Franciscan church, was begun in 1250 apparently to plans by Nicola Pisano. It was enlarged and modified in 1338 by Scipione Bon. Romanesque-Gothic in style, the **facade** is divided into three parts by pilasters, with spires at the top. A statue by Alessandro Vittoria is set above the portal while the figures at the sides are by the School of Bon.

The **campanile** is next in height to that of San Marco and was built by the Celega in the 14th century. The **interior** of the church is Latin-cross in plan with twelve columns supporting tall arches set between the nave and the two side aisles. After the *Mausoleum of Titian*, note should be taken of the many fine works which enrich the church and make it perhaps the most famous place in Venice, after San Marco, and together with San Zanipolo the one containing the greatest number of the mortal remains of famous men. In the right aisle the *altar* by Longhena has two statues by Giusto Le Court; in the second bay is *Titian's tomb* (the artist died of the plague in 1576), made in 1852 by pupils of Antonio Canova. The third altar has sculpture by Alessandro Vittoria. To the right of the right transept is the *Monument to Admiral Jacopo Marcello*, by Pietro Lombardo. On the wall next to it is the *Monument to the Blessed Pacifico* with a fine bas-relief (the *Baptism of Christ*) by Bartolo and Michele da Firenze. In the **Sacristy** there is a stupendous triptych by Giovanni Bellini depicting the *Enthroned Madonna and Child with Music-making Angels and Saints* (1488). In the third chapel of the right apse is a *triptych* by Bartolomeo

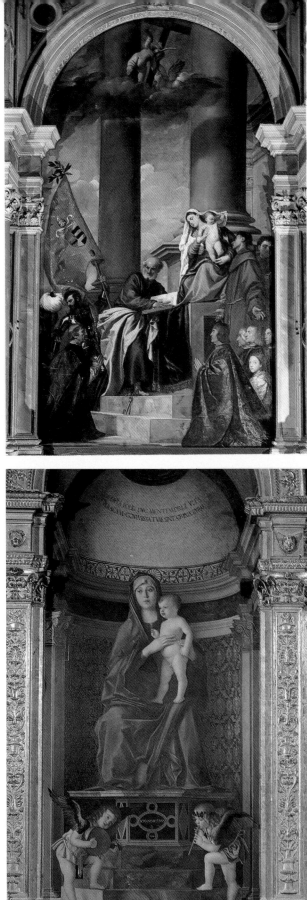

The church of Santa Maria Gloriosa dei Frari houses true masterpieces of Venetian painting: the Assumption and the Madonna of Ca' Pesaro, both by Titian, and Giovanni Bellini's Madonna.

Vivarini.

The *Monument to Doge Francesco Foscari*, by the Bregno brothers (circa 1475), is in the chancel; on the left wall is the *Monument to Doge Nicolò Tron* by Antonio Rizzo. Behind the high altar rises the famous *Assumption* by Titian (1518). Of note in the first apse chapel to the left is a lovely *Madonna and Child* (1535) by Bernardo Licinio. In the third chapel is an altarpiece by Alvise Vivarino and Marco Basaiti with *St. Ambrose Enthroned*. In the fourth, particular attention goes to a *triptych* by Bartolomeo Vivarini and a *St. John Baptist* by Jacopo Sansovino on the baptismal font.

In the left aisle, on the second altar, is the *Madonna di Casa Pesaro*, an altarpiece by Titian (1526) with, further on, the *Monument to Doge Giovanni Pesaro*, by Longhena (1669) and the *Mausoleum to Antonio Canova*, planned by the master and executed by his pupils.

SCUOLA GRANDE DI SAN ROCCO

All the most famous architects of the time had a hand in the building of the Scuola Grande di San Rocco, erected between 1515 and 1560. These included Bartolomeo Bon who designed it, Sante Lombardo, Scarpagnino, and finally Giangiacomo dei Grigi responsible for the finishing touches. The results of this composite work owe much to the style of Scarpagnino, who also created the fine pedimented portal and the magnificent staircase in the ground floor hall. Otherwise the **interior** is a monument to the art of Jacopo Tintoretto — whose original decoration is still in place — with his breathtakingly beautiful cycle of paintings. The decoration of the Hostel began in 1564; in the Great Hall the artist painted twenty-one canvases for the ceiling in panels. Eight large canvases, painted between 1583 and 1587, are in the large ground floor hall, divided by two rows of Corinthian columns into three aisles. Titian's *Annunciation* is particularly lovely. The **Chancellor's Office** also has an *Ecce Homo* attributed to Titian and a *Saint Rocco* by Bernardo Strozzi.

The facade of the Scuola Grande di San Rocco and, below, the church of the same name.

Left, a view of the Rio San Trovaso, and, on the right, the Rio delle Torreselle with the back of the Palazzo Dario.

The facade of the church of Santa Maria della Visitazione, begun in 1493 and terminated in 1524, is attributed to Mauro Colussi and also to Tullio Lombardo.

CHURCH OF SAN ROCCO

The church of San Rocco is right next to the Scuola Grande. It was rebuilt by Scalfarotto in the 18th century on the old Renaissance church. The **facade**, which echoes the motives of the Scuola, is decorated with statues by Morlaiter and Marchiori and has a fine portal with a gable.

The **interior**, with a single nave and side chapels and a dome over the sanctuary, houses a series of works by Tintoretto — two of the most outstanding are *St. Rocco Healing the Plague-stricken* and *St. Rocco in the Desert* —, by Pordenone, *St. Martin and St. Cristopher*, and fine frescoes. The relics of the Saint are in the sanctuary in an urn with a statue of *St. Rocco* above.

CHURCH OF SAN TROVASO

« *Trovaso* » is the contraction in dialect of Gervasio and Protasio. The Church of San Trovasio, already extant in the 11th century, was damaged by fire and rebuilt in 1590 in classical forms with two tiers of pilasters on the **facade**.

The Latin-cross **interior** has a nave only and contains important works by Pietro Lombardo, Domenico Tintoretto, Michele Giambono, Jacopo Tintoretto, Palma Giovane and Rosalba Carriera.

SQUERO OF SAN TROVASO

Near the **Church of San Trovaso** is the *squero* or private dockyard for the construction of ships, also called San Trovaso.

The picturesque group of buildings, some of which are in brick and some of wood, faces on the rio with a landing for the launching and the beaching of small vessels. It is here in fact that new gondolas are built and repairs are carried out. This is the only one of the many squeri once active in the city which still continues the centuries-old tradition of shipbuilding in the field of the typical Venetian craft.

The Church and the "squero" of San Trovaso.

The squero dates to the 17th century and the layout is basically still what it was, despite periodical renovation, with its small juxtaposed buildings, some serving as workshops, some as dwellings. A characteristic feature are the small houses on the landing with wooden balconies and railings and roofing supported by poles.

THE GONDOLA

The history of this slender boat, traditionally used by the dwellers of the lagoon, is a thousand years old. Said to date to the times of the first doge in the 7th century, the gondola is actually nominated for the first time in a public document of 1094. The origin of the name itself is uncertain and may, rather symbolically, come from the Greek *kondyle*, or « shell », or from *kondoura*, a sort of vessel, or from the Latin *cymbula*, or « small boat ». The gondolas built by the Venetian master hewers according to a tradition that was handed down orally were not always as they are today. Those depicted in 15th and 16th-century paintings were flatter bottomed and the stern and prow were not as high. The planking was brightly painted and decorated with costly appliqués, and the various noble families vied with each other in showing off their wealth. The two parts of the boat where the craftsmen's fancy was given free rein were the prow, rather like a halberd with six teeth (one for each sestriere in Venice), and the volute of the stern. In the 18th century the gondola was standardized (once some were larger, propelled by several oars) and it is now 10.75 m. Iong and 1.75 m. wide. The flat-bottomed boat is asymmetrical because it is propelled by a single oar on the starboard side. The gondolier, whose « uniform » consists of a striped jersey and a beribboned straw hat, was once much more curiously and elegantly outfitted. Standing on a small platform in the stern he pushes the gondola with his single long oar which rests on the typically curved rowlock or *forcola*. Ever since 1562 when the Senate of the Serenissima emanated a decree that put an end to the ostentatious ornamentation in which one family tried to outdo the other the gondolas have been black. The only space left for decorative invention is in the panels which cover the prow, sometimes carved with plant scrolls or — more rarely — with detailed views of the lagoon. Nor does the *felze*, a moveable arched shelter that formed a sort of cabin at the center of the boat to shield the passengers in bad weather, still exist. This hood, consisting of black cloth ornamented with cords and ribbons, had tiny windows and a small shuttered door.
The gondolas which now ply the Venetian waterways, barely one twentieth of those there in the 18th century, are built and repaired at the Squero di San Trovaso, where the artisans still keep the ancient craft alive.

CANAL AND ISLAND OF THE GIUDECCA

The entrance to the Giudecca Canal is right across from the island of San Giorgio. For centuries the canal has been the center for commerce and maritime trade in Venice and still today it is a large port where passenger ships dock. The mixture of ancient houses and small palaces in a variety of styles alternating with warehouses where modest artisans ply their trade gives meaning to what can then be encountered, on a larger scale, in the city. Outstanding among the more important buildings are the unusual silhouettes of the former **Stucky Mill**, the ex-**Church of S. Cosma e Damiano** and, above all, the churches of the **Zitelle** and of the **Redentore**, fine examples of the sculptural quality of the Baroque. Originally this small island went by the name of Spinalonga, and it was later called Giudecca, probably on account of the large number of Jews who settled here (14th-15th cent.), but this is no more than a hypothesis. It was once much smaller but as time went by reclamation and consolidation of the land turned it into what it is now.

Exterior of the church of San Barnaba.

A view of the canal of the Giudecca.

CHURCH OF SAN GIORGIO MAGGIORE

San Giorgio Maggiore is one of Andrea Palladio's finest works (1565-1580).

The **facade** is tripartite with columns and Corinthian capitals. The statues of *St. George* and *St. Stephen* are set into the two niches between the columns. In the wings are the *busts* by Giulio dal Moro. The **campanile** of 1791 is by Benedetto Buratti and was built to replace the one that fell in 1773.

The inverted Latin-cross interior has a nave and two aisles and a dome. Two splendid works by Tintoretto, a *Last Supper* and the *Gathering of the Manna*, are in the sanctuary. In the apse are fine wooden *choir stalls* of 1598 carved by the Flemish sculptor Van der Brulle.

GIORGIO CINI FOUNDATION

The former **Benedictine monastery on the island of San Giorgio**, dating far back in time, was restored and in 1957 became the headquarters of the Giorgio Cini Foundation, one of the most prestigious centers of culture and art in the world, the setting for innumerable international congresses and even summit meetings of heads of state. The monastery, unbelievably beautiful in the perfection of its Palladian architecture, includes among its many works of art a *Marriage of the Virgin* by Tintoretto.

Two pictures of the church of San Giorgio Maggiore.

MUSEUMS AND GALLERIES

GALLERIA DELL'ACCADEMIA

For a general view of the development of Venetian painting in the five centuries ranging from the 14th to the 18th century a visit to the Academy Gallery is essential. It was officially created as an « Accademia dei pittori e scultori » by a decree of the Republic of Venice on September 14, 1750. The first director was Giambattista Piazzetta and the headquarters were in the building which currently houses the Capitaneria di Porto. In 1807 it was decided to move it to the buildings of the Church of Santa Maria della Carità, the Scuola Grande of the same name, and the Monastero dei Canonici Lateranensi, forming the new « Accademia delle Belle Arti ». The old **Scuola della Confraternita** had been completed between the 14th and the 15th centuries. The facade was now renovated by Maccarozzi in neoclassic style on a project by Giorgio Massari. The **Church of Santa Maria della Carità** was on the site of a precedent Romanesque structure; the workshop of Bartolomeo Bon was involved in the new structure which dates to between 1441 and 1452. The third building, the **Convent of the Lateran Canons**, is one of the finest examples of Palladian architecture in Venice. These buildings were adapted to their new function by Antonio Selva who had what was left of the Corinthian atrium and the short sides of the cloister torn down, replacing them with a double loggia so as to connect the rooms of the convent with those of the church.

The original core of the present collection dates to the 18th century and was comprised of the paintings submitted by the aspiring academicians. From the time of its refounding one donation followed the other, both by private individuals — in particular the Contarini bequest of 1838 and the Renier legacy of 1850 — and the « forced » donations of the religious institutions repressed by Napoleon, as well as additions, in more recent times, due to acquisitions on the part of the State. An important group of paintings, chosen by Peter Edwards, president of the old Accademia from 1793-1796, was bought in 1812. Works by Carpaccio, the Bellinis, Titian, Pordenone, and Paolo Veronese were acquired in the years immediately after. When Napoleon fell, the Louvre had to return works by Paris Bordone, Jacopo Tintoretto, and the *Supper in the House of Levi* which Paolo Veronese had painted in 1537 for the Refectory of the Convent of Santi Giovanni e Paolo.

As already stated, the rooms provide a complete panorama of Venetian painting, beginning with works still of Byzantine inspiration. This period, up to the 14th century, is well represented by examples which include polyptychs by the Veneziano's — Catarino's *Coronation of the Virgin* dating to 1375, and the *Annunciation, Saints and Prophets* by Lorenzo of 1357. There are also works by Iacobello del Fiore, Iacobello Alberegno and Nicolo di

Pietro.

The 15th century is also represented by outstanding paintings, including Giovanni Bellini's *Madonna and Child between St. Catherine and the Magdalen*, *Enthroned Madonna Adoring the Sleeping Child in her Lap*, and the entire cycle of the *Legend of St. Orsola* by Carpaccio, originally painted for the oratory of the Scuola di Sant'Orsola. There are also numerous works by Vivarini, G. D'Alemagna, Lazzaro Bastiani.

For the 16th century of particular note is Giorgione's most famous painting, *The Tempest*, as well as what remains of his fresco showing a *Nude* that originally decorated the facade of the Fondaco dei Tedeschi. Then there is Titian's *Pietà* and his *Presentation of the Virgin in the Temple*, Paolo Veronese's *Supper in the House of Levi* and his *Madonna and Child with Saints*, as well as the stupendous *Miracle of St. Mark* and *Adam and Eve* by Jacopo Tintoretto. There is also a rich assortment of works by minor artists, Boccaccino, Lorenzo Lotto, Paris Bordone, Schiavone, Pordenone.

◄ *Francesco Guardi: The Island of San Giorgio Maggiore.*

Giovanni da Bologna: Madonna of Humility.

Paolo Veneziano: Madonna Enthroned.

Niccolò di Pietro: Enthroned Madonna and Child with Patron.

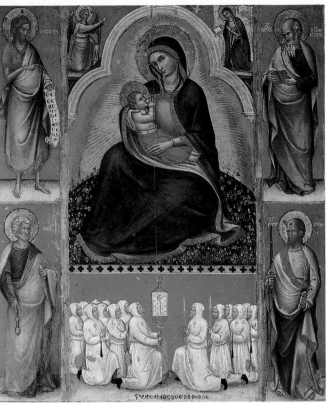

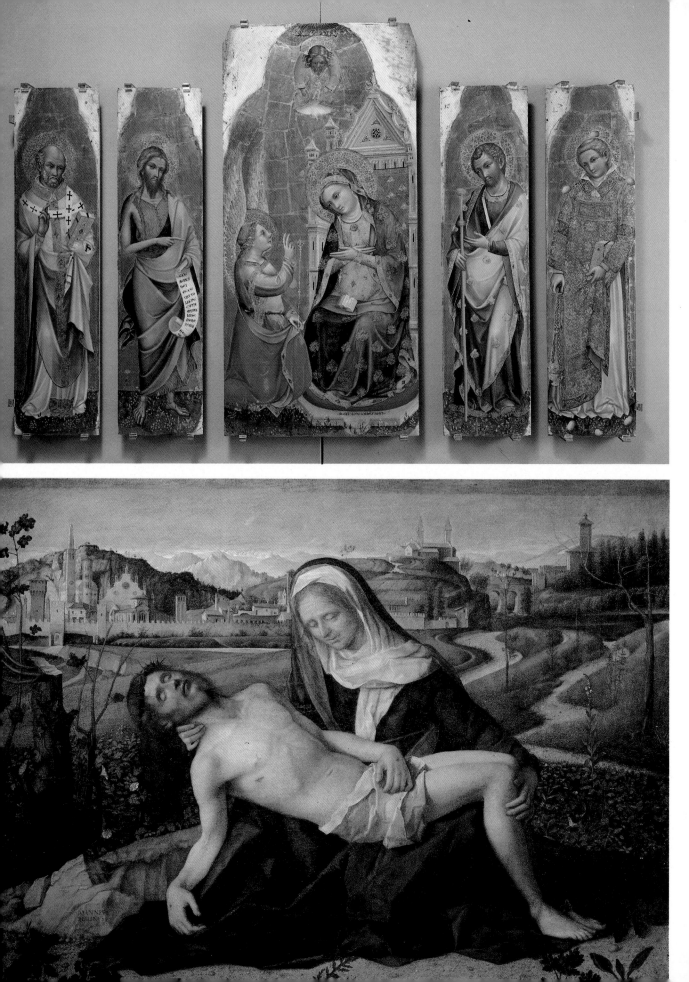

◄ *Lorenzo Veneziano: Polyptych with the Annunciation and four Saints.*

◄ *Giovanni Bellini: Pietà.*

Gentile Bellini: Healing of Pietro de' Ludovici.

Giorgione (Giorgio da Castelfranco): The Tempest.

Bonifacio de' Pitati: The Rich Man's Feast.

Andrea Mantegna: St. George.

Palma il Vecchio: Assumption.

Works by Bernardo Strozzi, *Banquet in the House of the Pharisee* and *Saint Jerome*; the *Parable of the Good Samaritan* by Domenico Fetti; Mazzoni's *Annunciation*, as well as paintings by Marrei and others cover the 17th century.

The 18th century is particularly well represented, with some of the most important works of Venetian artists, including Pietro Longhi's *Philosopher*, the *Fortune-teller* and a *Crucifixion* by G. B. Piazzetta, *Portrait of a Young Man* and a *Self-Portrait* by Rosalba Carriera, *St. Joseph with the Child and other Saints* by G. B. Tiepolo, and finally Canaletto's *Porticato*.

◄ *Canaletto: Portico*

Titian: Pietà

Tintoretto (Jacopo Robusti): Saint Mark Saves a Saracen.

◄ Gentile Bellini: Miracles of the Holy Cross,
The Holy Cross Fallen into the Canal of San Lorenzo.

◄ Vittore Carpaccio: the Healing of a Lunatic.

Vittore Carpaccio: Legend of Saint Orsola (detail). The English
Ambassadors Presenting the Proposal of Marriage to King
Maurus of Brittany.

◄ *G. B. Piazzetta: The Fortune-teller.*

◄ *Rosalba Carriera: Self-portrait.*

◄ *Francesco Guardi: Fire at S. Marcuola.*

The ball-room with frescoes by G. Crosato.

MUSEO DEL SETTECENTO VENEZIANO

The Museum of the Venetian Eighteenth Century is in **Palazzo Rezzonico** in the sestriere of Dorsoduro.

In 1935 the palace was bought by the City of Venice which restored and refurbished the interior as a splendid aristocratic Venetian 18th-century home.

The **Ballroom** — entrance to which is via a *staircase* by G. Massari — with stupendous carved furniture by Brustolon, leads to the **Room of the Allegory of Marriage**, named after the fresco by Tiepolo depicting the *Wedding of Ludovico Rezzonico*, from the **Room of the Pastels** with works by Rosalba Carriera, to the **Hall of Tapestries**, with 17th-century Flemish *tapestries*; from the **Throne Room**, formerly nuptial chamber with a fresco by Tiepolo, to the Hall dedicated to him where he painted the large fresco with *Fortune* and *Wisdom*: from the **Library Hall** with *canvases of mythological subjects* by Maffei to the **Sala del Lazzarini** and that of Brustolon with beautiful pieces of inlaid furniture made by the master from Belluno who was particularly active in Venice.

On the second floor the **Portego dei Dipinti**, with works by Piazzetta, Jan Liss and Giuseppe Zais, leads to the **Sala del Longhi** with 34 pictures of *life in Venice*. The *ceiling* is by Tiepolo. After two smaller rooms, frescoed by Guardi, comes the perfect reconstruction of an 18th-century bedroom. Two more small rooms, and the visitor finds himself in a reconstruction of the villa at Zianigo with frescoes by Gian Domenico Tiepolo.

Of particular interest on the second floor are the **Room of the Clowns**, the **Chapel** frescoed by Tiepolo in 1749, and the **Sala del Ridotto** (Gaming room) with the famous small paintings by Guardi, the *Parlatorio delle Monache* (*Nuns' Parlor*) and the *Sala del Ridotto*.

The small **Room of the Stuccoes** is particularly charming. Just as interesting on the third floor is the reconstruction of an old pharmacy or Chemist's Shop and a Marionette Theater, with a collection of 18th-century Venetian marionettes.

119

The Sala del Tiepolo.

Francesco Guardi: Piazzetta San Marco (Galleria Franchetti). ▶

Francesco Guardi: Grand Canal with the church of the Santa ▶
Maria of the Salute (Galleria Franchetti).

GALLERIA FRANCHETTI

The collection is situated on the upper floors of the **Ca' d'Oro**, and to get there one must first cross a fine courtyard — entrance to which is from the Grand Canal, through a lovely Gothic four-light opening — embellished by a 15th-century marble *well-head* before climbing an open staircase resting on Gothic arches. The ground floor portico is surrounded by various Roman and Hellenistic *statues* and has a mosaic pavement. The **Quadreria** (Picture Gallery) displays works by Antonio Vivarini, Vittore Carpaccio, Paris Borbone, Alessandro Vittoria, Titian, Mantegna — his splendid painting of *St. Sebastian* —, Van Dyck, Pontormo, Filippo Lippi, Fran-

cesco Guardi, Luca Signorelli, Van Eyck, Tintoretto, Sansovino. The Gallery now also contains the frescoes by Campagnola and Pordenone which were removed from the walls of the cloister of Santo Stefano, as well as old Venetian ceramics from the 11th to the 18th centuries including the famous fragments of the Conton collection. Other rooms annexed to the Gallery belong to the Palazzo Giusti, which is next to the Ca' d'Oro. These three rooms contain bronzes of Venetian school and other examples of Flemish and Dutch art. Note should be taken in passing from the first to the second floor of the Ca' d'Oro of a splendid carved wooden *staircase*, originally in the Agnello House.

PINACOTECA QUERINI STAMPALIA

The Querini Stampalia Collection of Paintings is housed in the palace of that name behind the Church of Santa Maria Formosa, next to the rich private library donated to the city by Count Querini Stampalia.

The Picture Gallery consists of twenty rooms, on the second floor, which contain furniture, porcelains, arms and musical instruments as well as works by artists active between the 14th and 18th centuries.

The most interesting paintings include a *Self-Portrait* and *Adam and Eve* by Palma Giovane, the *Conversion of St. Paul* by Andrea Schiavone, an *Adoration of the Madonna* by Lorenzo di Credi, a *Sacra Conversazione* by Palma Vecchio, *Hunting in the Valley* by Pietro Longhi — the museum owns a rich collection of works by this artist —, various landscapes by Marco Ricci, the *Portrait of G. Querini* by G. B. Tiepolo and a *Madonna and Child* by Bernardo Strozzi.

Various rooms in the gallery still have their original 18th-century furnishings, with splendid Chinese lacquer furniture, Louis XVI mirrors, stucco decoration. Also to be noted are drawings by Giovanni Bellini, Titian, Raphael, Tintoretto and Veronese.

Exterior of Palazzo Querini Stampalia.

Palazzo Querini Stampalia: the Green Drawing-room, in Venetian Baroque style of the 18th century.

MUSEO CIVICO CORRER

The Museo Civico Correr is situated in the **Napoleonic Wing of the Procuratie Nuove**. Formed around an original nucleus of paintings given in 1830 by the Venetian patrician Teodoro Correr. The entire conspicuous patrimony of the Correr collection has been divided into three sections, two of which are installed elsewhere: the Museum of the Venetian Eighteenth Century (Settecento) in Ca' Rezzonico and the Archaeological Museum in another wing of the Procuratie Nuove with an entrance from the Piazzetta. The Museo Correr is dedicated to the Historical Collections, the Picture Gallery and the Museum of the Risorgimento. The **Historical Collections** are spread out over thirty-three rooms, on the first floor, in which an astounding variety of objects is on display, furnishing as complete a picture as possible of the social life, the institutions of art and history of the Most Serene Republic. Included in this wide array of precious objects are various representations of the Lion of St. Mark, symbols and banners of the Serenissima, coats of arms and portraits of the doges, their seals, the costumes of the doge and other high magistrates, depictions of public ceremonies, mementos of the famous plot of Bajamonte Tiepolo, an important coin collection, illustrations of ships and naval documents, keepsakes of the Battle of Lepanto, nautical maps and navigator's instruments, the map of the colonial conquests, weapons, flags, coats of arms, staffs of command and trophies, as well as Antonio Canova's early masterpiece, *Daedalus and Icarus*.

The **Picture Gallery (Quadreria)** is installed in nineteen rooms on the second floor. In the first and second of these are examples of Venetian-Byzantine art and works by 16th-century Venetian painters; outstanding is Paolo Veneziano. The third room features the works of Lorenzo Veneziano while of particular note in the next room dedicated to flamboyant Gothic are the 14th-century panels and the sculpture by Jacopo delle Masegne. The fifth room contains Late Gothic Venetian painting, which reappears in the sixth room featuring works by Jacobello del Fiore and Michele Giambono.

The greatest masterpieces of the Ferrarese artist Cosme Tura (note the splendid *Pietà*) are collected in the seventh room, which also contains works by other artists from Ferrara and two *Madonnas* by Bartolomeo Vivarini. The following rooms are dedicated to Venetian wood sculpture and works by artists of the Flemish school including an *Adoration of the Magi* by Peter Brueghel. Further on, one of the rooms has a *Pietà* by Antonello della Messina, a *Crucifixion* by Hugo van der Goes and a *Madonna and Child* by Bouts. Cranach, Bruyn and il Civetta are present in the twelfth room while the following room boasts paintings by Giovanni, Jacopo and Gentile Bellini. Alvise Vivarini and the artists close to him appear in the fourteenth room. Vittore Carpaccio's *Courtesans* and other works by the same artist cover the space of two rooms while the seventeenth contains Lorenzo Lotto's *Madonna and Child Crowned by Angels*. In the eighteenth are to be found examples of the work of the famous « Madonneri », Greek-Venetian painters of the 16th and 17th centuries. Examples of 16th-century ceramics are on exhibit in the last room of the Picture Gallery. Particularly admired is the famous « Correr dinner service » consisting of seventeen pieces decorated by Niccolo Pellipario in 1525.

Anonymous 17th-century painter: Allegory of the Holy Alliance (Museo Correr).

Vittore Carpaccio: The Visitation (Museo Correr).

MURANO

This typical settlement in the lagoon spreads out over five islands and was created by refugees from Opiterga and Altino fleeing from the Huns and Lombards. It developed rapidly and as early as 1275 was already governed by a Venetian podestà but with regulations of its own. For centuries it was considered the vacation site for the patrician families of Venice, and as a result churches and palaces were built and rebuilt.

Glass making, for which Murano has become famous throughout the world, has ancient beginnings. In 1292 all the glass factories of Venice were transferred to Murano so as to protect the city from the danger of fire. With the affirmation of blown glass and the development of other techniques such as milk glass, Murano reached its zenith in the 15th century.

Only a few of the many outstanding palaces are cited. The **Palazzo Da Mula**, a fine Gothic building, stands next to the **Ponte Vivarini**; the **Palazzo Trevisan**, attributed to Palladio, is no less interesting. On the opposite shore is the **Museo dell'Arte Vetraria**, or Glass Museum, in the former **Palazzo Giustinian**. Of particular interest are the churches: the most famous is **SS. Maria e Donato**.

Glass-blowing in Murano.

The apse of the church of SS. Maria e Donato.

BURANO

The original settlement of Burano was on a different island, closer to the sea, and it was probably due to some natural calamity that the community of Burano later moved to « *Vicus Buranis* », on the island near Mazzorbo. Life on the island, which counted about 8,000 souls, was bound to Torcello up to the 18th century, when Torcello went into its fatal decline. Life on Burano was always characterized by its relation with art. The musician B. Galuppi was born here in 1706 and it was a fertile point of encounter for painters above all in the 20th century.

The most important economic activity of Burano is a felicitous encounter of art and craft: the lace which reached its zenith between the 16th and 17th centuries, thanks also to the protection granted by the Dogaresses Giovanna Duodo and Morosina Morosini. There was a decline in lace-making in the 18th century until a school was established in the 1880s and 90s.

There are two churches on the island: the church of **San Martino** founded in the 16th century and the church of **Santa Maria delle Grazie**, set on the site of a chapel of Doge Grimani.

The famous lace of Burano.

A typical corner of Burano.

The cathedral of Torcello dedicated to Santa Maria Assunta.

A typical canal and the church of Santa Fosca. ▶

TORCELLO

Torcello is one of the loveliest islands in the lagoon thanks to its aura of times past.

It was one of the most important islands in the history of the early settlements and became bishop's seat in the 7th century when it had a much larger population than the barely one hundred souls who live there now.

In 1247 Torcello had its own statute and a podestà, trade was lively and churches and palaces were being built. The malaria which spread as the result of the deviation of the mouth of the Stile marked the end of life on the island. The **Cathedral of Santa Fosca** is a building of the year thousand which betrays the influence of Ravenna in its octagonal ground plan with a portico on five sides. The Greek-cross interior is highly impressive. The **Cathedral of Santa Maria Assunta** was founded in 639 and partly rebuilt in 1008, and is the finest example of the artistic influence of Ravenna, through which Byzantine art arrived in the lagoon. Inside is a 12th-13th-century Venetian-Byzantine mosaic, with the *Last Judgement*; the *iconostasis* or rood screen with marble columns and thirteen *icons* of the early 15th century; the altar with a *Roman sarcophagus* from Altino under the altar table, and a *Madonna and Child*, a 13th-century mosaic in Venetian style, while the *Apostles* are 12th-century Ravennate in style. The *crypt* dates to the 9th century. These are the most important works in the cathedral. Behind the church is the **Chapel of San Marco** where it is said the relics of the Evangelist stopped on their way to Venice. Little remains of the **Baptistry** that once stood facing the church. Archaeological finds and evidence of the history of Torcello and the lagoon as well as works of art and paintings are installed in the **Museo dell'Estuario** in the **Palazzo del Consiglio** and in the **Palazzo dell'Archivio** (which also has early-Veneto, Etruscan, and Greek finds); both dating to the 14th century. Only a few vestiges of the **Palazzo del Podestà** are still extant (plaques, coats of arms, column fragments).

CONTENTS